The **V** ... **BOUT** ... **dbook**

"If you're looking for a bottom-dollar flight, courier trips can't be beat. For valuable information, check out *The Courier Air Travel Handbook* by Mark Field."
— *Cosmopolitan Magazine*

"*The Courier Air Travel Handbook* will help you stretch your travel budget."
— *Off Duty Military Magazine*

"Fly to Worldwide Destinations for as little as $99 roundtrip, or even free."
— *Transitions Abroad Magazine*

"The Courier's Bible . . ."
— *The Midwest Book Review*

"To sort out fact from fiction about courier travel, get *The Courier Air Travel Handbook*."
— *The Houston Chronicle*

"The courier company pays most or all of your airfare."
— *The Seattle Times*

"Colossal savings on airfare are offered to air couriers."
— *Fodor's Travel Publications*

"Go as a courier, and save major bucks on a flight."
— *Newsday*

"This book explains how you can fly around the world for next to nothing."
— *The Arizona Republic*

"As a courier, fly three times as far at about 25 percent of the cost. The bargains are extreme."
— *The San Francisco Chronicle*

"A handy guide to the ins and outs of courier travel is *The Courier Air Travel Handbook* by Mark I. Field."
— *The Chicago Sun Times*

Timeless Travel Quotes

I travel not to go anywhere, but to go. I travel for travel's sake. The great affair is to move.

—Robert Louis Stevenson
1850–1894

Travel, in the younger sort, is a part of education; in the elder, a part of experience.

—Francis Bacon
1561–1626

Travel is one way of lengthening life, at least in appearance.

—Benjamin Franklin
1706–1790

Il faut être toujours botté et prêt à partir. (One should always have one's boots on and be ready to leave.)

—Michel de Montaigne
1533–1592

THE
COURIER AIR TRAVEL
HANDBOOK

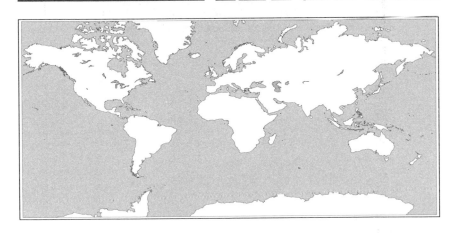

Learn How to Travel Worldwide for Next to Nothing

Mark I. Field

**Perpetual Press
Seattle, Washington**

Field Travel Guides
An Innovative Travel Series

The Courier Air Travel Handbook

Printed in the United States of America
Book-cover design by Bob Silverman
Interior design and layout by Julia M. Lauer, Tammy Thornas, Brenda Spoonemore, and Andrew Ratshin
Cover photos courtesy of Andy M. Clarke and Kristen C. Weiss

First printing–July 1990
Second printing–August 1991–2nd edition
Third printing–November 1991
Fourth printing–December 1991
Fifth printing–February 1992
Sixth printing–May 1992–3rd edition
Seventh printing–October 1992
Eighth printing–May 1993
Ninth printing–October 1993–4th edition
Tenth printing–June 1994
Eleventh printing–February 1996–5th edition
Twelfth printing–June 1996–6th edition

ISBN 1-881199-35-5

Published by:
Perpetual Press
P.O. Box 45628
Seattle, Washington 98145-0628

Distributed to the Book Trade by:
Ingram Book Company at (800) 937-8000

Published in Europe by Uitgeverij Het Spectrum BV.

ABOUT THE AUTHOR

Mark I. Field is an avid world traveler. He is originally from New York City and now makes his home in Arizona, where he is a newspaper publisher. Prior to attending college, he spent eight years in the Navy serving on submarines, where he was part of the Space Shuttle Challenger Recovery Operation and served in Military Intelligence. He is a graduate of the University of Arizona with a degree in business economics and attended The American Graduate School of International Management.

Mark was inspired to write this book because during his travels he encountered so many people who knew little or nothing about courier travel. He felt more people would have the opportunity to travel if they only knew about this concept. "The ability to travel should not be decided by one's financial position," he asserts. On one of his trips Mark backpacked throughout Europe on an extremely limited budget . . . and had the time of his life. Besides travel, Mark also enjoys basketball, golf, and tennis.

Dedication

This book is dedicated to my mother, Betty Lou Field, who inspired in me a desire to travel and see the world.

Acknowledgments

The author wishes to thank the following people:

- ♦ Julia M. Lauer for her creative ability.
- ♦ Jeffrey J. Leslie for his continued support and assistance.
- ♦ Dan Poynter for his inspiration and guidance.
- ♦ Tammy Thornas for her commitment and tireless dedication.
- ♦ Kristen C. Weiss for her exceptional research and marketing ability.
- ♦ Craig Evans for his outstanding research dedication.
- ♦ Heidi Robinson for her thorough proof-reading and layout support.
- ♦ Jennifer DuBois and Thom Votteler for project management.

Contents

A Note on Prices and Destinations

The courier industry, like the travel industry, changes constantly. Every effort has been made to provide the reader with accurate information, and all the information in this book is based on the best information available at the time of publication.

This book is updated at each printing. This ensures the most current information is available to the reader. This sixth edition is completely revised from cover to cover.

Prices, destinations, phone numbers, and other pertinent information in this book are subject to change. It is important to realize that courier companies may go out of business, change their policies concerning onboard couriers, or simply change their phone numbers.

If you come across any new information, please write to me in care of the publisher. If I include it in the next edition of this book, I will acknowledge your contribution and send you a free copy of the book.

—*Mark I. Field*

COMMON QUESTIONS AND ANSWERS ABOUT COURIER TRAVEL

Q: Who can travel as a courier?

A: Anyon who is over the age of 18 and has a valid passport. You need not be a citizen of the country in which the courier flights originate. If you are a traveler, student, teacher, retiree, businessperson, adventurer, or just interested in saving money, you're an ideal candidate for courier travel.

Q: Will I have to transport anything illegal?

A: Absolutely not. The courier industry is a respectable industry.

Q: What will I have to transport?

A: The types of items that you will transport include documents, files, boxes, computer disks, contracts, and so on. You will *not* have to load the material. The courier company takes care of that on both ends.

Q: What are the benefits of courier travel?

A: The money you save. As a courier, you will only pay a small percentage of the cost of the plane ticket.

Q: Can I pay the airline money to take an extra bag?

A: Most airlines will allow you to take extra baggage if you pay an additional baggage charge, but it may or may not be worth the extra money. If you must take your entire wardrobe, then courier travel may not be for you. In that case, give this book to a friend!

WORLDWIDE COURIER DESTINATIONS

1. Abu Dhabi	12. Brussels	23. Frankfurt
2. Accra	13. Budapest	24. Gabarone
3. Amsterdam	14. Buenos Aires	25. Geneva
4. Athens	15. Cairo	26. Harare
5. Atlanta	16. Caracas	27. Helsinki
6. Auckland	17. Chicago	28. Hong Kong
7. Bahrain	18. Copenhagen	29. Honolulu
8. Bangkok	19. Dallas	30. Houston
9. Barcelona	20. Detroit	31. Johannesburg
10. Berlin	21. Dubai	32. Jamaica
11. Boston	22. Dublin	33. London

HOW TO USE THIS GUIDE

NEW YORK

Air Facility

Destination	R/T fare	Last-minute fare	Length of stay/Departure days
Caracas	$210	$100	6–7 days Tue–Fri, Sat
Madrid	$350	$180	Varies
Mexico City	$200	$100	Varies
Rio de Janiero	$480	$300	8, 9, or 14 days Tue, Wed, Sat
Sao Paulo	$340	$180	Varies

Flights originating from: New York
Address: 153-40 Rockaway Boulevard
City/State/Zip: Jamaica, NY 11434
Phone: 718-712-1769
Fax: 718-712-1574
Toll-free number: No
Point of contact: Claudio, Ruth, or Alex
Times to call: 11AM–5PM EST Mon–Fri
Recorded information: No
Type of business: Courier company
Conducting business since: 1988
Annual registration fee: No
Courier assignment length: One–two weeks
Luggage restrictions: Carry-on only
Frequent flyer mileage accrued: No
Airlines used: Varig, LanChile, United, Ladeco
Return date flexibility: No
One-way tickets available: No
Cancellation phone list: Yes
Last-minute discounts: Yes
Additional non-courier travel services: No
Recommended advance reservations: One month
Earliest possible reservations: Three months
Departure taxes: $28
Deposit: No
Method of payment: Certified check, money order, cash, personal check
Credit cards accepted: No
Comments: Prices are slightly higher during summer months. Air Facility depends on responsible people to act as couriers for them. If you cancel a flight last minute, they place you on a black list, and you will not be allowed to fly with them in the future. They are helpful and offer consistently inexpensive fares to South America.

Courier company name: The name under which the company conducts business
Destination: Cities to which the company offers courier flights
R/T fare: Standard round-trip fare offered by the courier company
Last minute fare: Cheapest fare; flight usually departs in a couple days
Length of stay/Departure days: Information concerning how long the trip is and which days flights depart
Flights originating from: Cities from which the courier flights originate
Address: Location from which this office conducts business
City/State/Zip: City, state, and zip code from which this office conducts business
Phone: Phone number at which to call courier company
Fax: Fax number at which to fax courier company
Toll-free number: Toll free number at which to call the company
Point of contact: Person to contact to help arrange courier flights
Times to call: General business hours or specific times outlined by the courier company
Recorded information: Recorded phone message providing courier flight availability, fares, and other information
Type of business: Courier company, courier broker, or travel agent
Conducting business since: Year in which the company began operations
Annual registration fee: Fee assigned by the courier company or broker
Courier assignment length: Length of stay

Luggage restrictions: Number of pieces of luggage allowed
Frequent flyer mileage accrued: Whether frequent flyer mileage goes to the traveler
Airlines used: Airlines that courier company flights are on
Return date flexibility: Whether you can change the return date
One-way tickets available: Restrictions of courier company concerning roundtrip or one way courier flights
Cancellation phone list: Whether the company will contact you if they have a cancellation
Last-minute discounts: Whether a company will offer a discounted fare covering flights with short notice
Additional non-courier travel services: Whether a company offers information on rental cars and other travel services
Recommend advance reservations: How far in advance you should call for your flight reservation
Earliest possible reservations: How far in advance you can call for your reservation
Departure taxes: Additional fees added to your courier flight
Deposit: Money courier companies ask you to put up to ensure you fulfill your obligation
Method of payment: How you can pay for your courier flight
Credit cards accepted: Whether the courier company will accept credit cards
Comments: Other miscellaneous information

PART I

ABOUT

COURIER TRAVEL

What is a courier? A courier is a person who delivers something for someone. Couriers purchase reduced rate airline tickets from courier companies in exchange for accompanying cargo on a commercial airline. An air courier is an individual such as yourself who acts as the agent simply by occupying a seat on the plane and therefore permits the courier company to transport packages by air. Federal Express, UPS, and Emery are examples of air courier companies; however, they are large and own their own planes. There are literally hundreds of such companies in the world, though most of them are lesser known than Federal Express and UPS. The air courier companies in this book solicit members of the public to act as couriers for them. By acting as an air courier you allow the company to transport material by giving up the right to check in some or all of your luggage in exchange for a cheaper airfare.

Every year thousands of people travel around the world as couriers. This book will show you step-by-step how to become an air courier. You can begin today to travel to many exciting cities around the world for a fraction of the normal cost of airline tickets. Courier travel is one of the cheapest and simplest ways to travel around the world. How else can you travel from New York to London for $99 roundtrip or Los Angeles to Hong Kong for $150 roundtrip? This book will show you how you can travel worldwide for next to nothing or even free.

WHO CAN TRAVEL AS AN AIR COURIER?

Courier travel is available to anyone, provided you are over the age of eighteen and have a valid passport. Courier travel is used by a wide variety of people, especially students, senior citizens, business travelers, adventurers, or just anyone interested in saving money. Senior citizens are becoming an increasingly important part of this industry, because many of them have the desire and time to travel. Courier travel is also an ideal method of travel for both students and teachers given their natural desire to travel and their ample free time.

WHAT DO COURIER COMPANIES SHIP?

First, courier companies will not attempt to ship anything illegal. The items that you will transport may include documents, books, blueprints, supplies, equipment, checks, and so on. The material is similar to material shipped via other sources, such as Federal Express or UPS. The items tend to be time-sensitive. Simply put, it needs to get there quickly. It is important to know that the courier company will turn the material over to the airline, and they will retrieve the material upon completion of the flight. You, the courier, will usually never see or touch the actual shipment. What you actually carry is a manifest, which is a detailed list of cargo that the courier company is shipping. This is what you present to the customs officer upon arrival in a foreign country. It is because you never touch the material, that you, the courier, need not be bonded. Occasionally, there is a need for bonded couriers to deliver high-value items; however, most bonded couriers are professionals in the industry and tend to do this on a full-time basis. If you are interested in this line of employment, you should make this known to the courier company. However, this book is oriented toward the nonprofessional, leisure, or business traveler. As stated before, the companies listed in this book do not require bonding.

WHY ARE COURIERS USED?

The use of courier companies is a cheaper and more efficient way to ship materials compared to traditional transportation methods, such as rail, truck, and air freight. The reason for this is that the courier companies ship the material as luggage on board commercial airlines. All passenger baggage is walked through customs, as opposed to unaccompanied shipments. This is the key behind courier travel.

Unaccompanied material can be detained by customs, often for over a week. This would add tremendous expense to the cost of transportation. Recently I sent a box of these books internationally through air freight, as opposed to using a courier service, only to have the books be delayed in storage by customs for ten days. Additionally, customs then charged the recipient of the books ten days worth of storage, which exceeded the cost of the shipment itself. Aside from the fact that the material shipped through courier companies tends to be cheaper for the consumer, it is also much more efficient for time-sensitive material. For example, daily sales reports might need to be transported from a branch office in New York to the firm's headquarters in London. Certain items cannot be faxed, such as original contracts, checks, and of course, bulky material.

One of my favorite examples of this is when a Hollywood film company was making a movie in London and left the lead actress's wig in Los Angeles. A courier company was used to transport the wig to London that same day. So you can see, there really is a need for courier service. Many people, including myself, have used this method of travel to see the world on a shoestring.

Often the courier company does not have anything to ship. This does not mean, however, that they do not still have a ticket to sell. Most courier companies buy their tickets for a flight every day for up to six months in advance. For example, one company in New York might purchase a ticket to Paris on an American Airlines flight that leaves at ten o'clock in the morning every day of the year. So if you buy a ticket for a flight to Paris three months in advance, the courier company will not know if they have anything to transport until a day or two before the flight. Even if the courier company has nothing to ship, the plane ticket has already been bought by the courier company and re-sold to you. This was the case on my recent flight to London. Given that my ticket only cost $250 roundtrip, I could not have gotten a better deal.

But why do courier companies need people to fly as couriers? All overseas flights must have a passenger for the checked luggage. This is a security issue. When you check in for a flight at Los Angeles International Airport or any other airport, the authorities check your baggage. The courier company must abide by these same rules.

You should be very careful when asked to transport a bag for somebody else, because you might not know what the contents may be. It is important to ensure that the material is thoroughly checked by the authorities and that you have a manifest. The courier company provides you with a manifest itemizing what is being transported.

Due to the fact that you will not touch the material, you are not responsible for it in case of damage during transport. It is the courier company's responsibility to ensure the material is packaged well and arrives intact. You are essentially just going along for the ride.

WILL I HAVE TO TRANSPORT ANYTHING ILLEGAL?

A bsolutely not. This is the most common question I am asked about courier travel. All over the world, people have concerns about this question. I personally have traveled as a courier, and have met many other people who have had only good experiences when using this book as a guide. The companies in this book are reputable, and are used by thousands of people each and every year.

Travel as an air courier is safe. You will not be transporting anything illegal; this is a very respectable industry. When you contact a courier company to inquire about a particular flight, not only will they inform you of the airline that you will travel with, but they will often include a letter from that airline, indicating that this courier company is either the exclusive courier agent or one of the courier agents used by that airline. Again, all of the courier companies listed in this book are legitimate and reputable. Furthermore, they must be insured and bonded to operate in this industry.

There has been some negative publicity surrounding the term "courier." This is a broad term applied to many things; unfortunately it is sometimes applied to drug and contraband smuggling. This is not the case for courier companies listed in this book. These companies are reputable firms in good standing with the airlines.

However, courier companies start up, change names, change ownership, change phone numbers, change policies regarding onboard couriers, and change prices and destinations. If you come across a new courier company—one that is not listed in this book—use common sense to determine if it is a legitimate company. As more businesses expand into the international market, the greater the necessity for courier companies and agents called couriers. Additionally, as the speed of communication increases, the speed of transportation must keep pace. This is why the courier industry is expanding.

WHAT ARE THE ECONOMICS OF COURIER TRAVEL?

T he economics behind the courier industry are quite simple. A courier company will purchase a roundtrip ticket in advance to an overseas destination. This ticket might cost the company $700 roundtrip. They, in turn, take orders to ship material for that day. A courier company will charge about $50 to deliver a small package overseas;

FLIGHT PRICE COMPARISON

Trip	Airlines		Courier	
	Advance Purchase	**Last Minute**	**Advance Purchase**	**Last Minute**
New York–Rome	$1100	$1400	$250	$99
Los Angeles–London	$975	$1950	$450	$200
Miami–Rio de Janeiro	$880	$1630	$475	$250
San Francisco–Bangkok	$1390	$1610	$420	$100
Los Angeles–Sydney	$890	$1900	$899	$399
Chicago–Mexico City	$280	$280	$199	$99
New York–London	$770	$1320	$200	$99
New York–Caracas	$525	$670	$249	$89
New York–Singapore	$1730	$1500	$699	$199
Miami–Madrid	$995	$1065	$375	$200
Miami–Mexico City	$440	$440	$250	$100
Los Angeles–Tokyo	$1365	$2055	$450	$100
San Francisco–Hong Kong	$880	$1040	$400	$100
Houston–London	$725	$1625	$299	$99
Toronto–London	$640	$1860	$525	$425
Montreal–Paris	$610	$2410	$395	$350
Vancouver–Hong Kong	$1195	$1180	$700	$200

large, heavy, or expensive items can be delivered for an even higher price. The courier could generate up to $4,000 in revenue per flight.

The company then turns around and sells you their $700 roundtrip ticket for as low as $99. According to this example, the company would bring in roughly $3,350 in profit. This is the reason why they can afford to sell you the plane ticket so inexpensively.

The courier company offers the plane ticket to the general public at a discounted price in order to recoup some of their money. If the courier company cannot sell the ticket, or if they have a cancellation, then the ticket may be given away for free. This happens fairly often, as it is better for the company to take a loss on the $700 ticket than to send an employee who would have to be paid for his time and expenses. Simply put, it is in the best interest of the courier company to offer the ticket for sale to the general public. There are times when some courier companies are unable to locate people able and willing to fly to a particular city on a certain date. This is when the courier companies become desperate and ticket prices drop considerably.

A good example of this is when World Courier could not locate anyone to fly to Mexico City, and was forced to offer the ticket for free for over a two-month period. Another example is New York to Singapore for $150 roundtrip.

The price you pay for your ticket is simply a supply and demand dilemma. For example, the demand for airline tickets to Greece in the summer is high, while the supply is fixed; therefore, the price will rise. This is true with courier companies, commercial airlines, and the travel industry in general. So if you want to take a courier flight in the summer time, expect prices to be higher due to the increased number of people interested in flying and willing to do it. It is unlikely you will find the greatest savings during the summer. This is also true during the holidays. If you want to fly to Paris for Christmas, courier flights will be at a premium. However, even though the prices will be high relative to courier travel, they will still be less than commercial flights.

One way I am able to work around this problem is by attempting to travel off-season. Instead of flying to Greece in the summer, consider going to South America or Asia. However, often one country's low season is another country's high-season, and you can use this to your advantage. Australia's peak season is December through March—their summer, and our winter. This time of year is also a slow time for people willing to travel, both in Europe and in the United States. Therefore, you can expect inexpensive airline tickets to Australia during its high season.

Traveling as a courier is similar to traveling as a full-paying passenger—the only difference is the access to the information in this book and the price you pay. Couriers are sent on major airlines including United, Northwest, Delta, American, British Airways, Virgin, Lufthansa, Air France, Iberia, Cathay Pacific, and Singapore Airlines. As an air courier, you will be treated like any other passenger. The only difference will be that the person sitting next to you might be paying $500 more for their seat than you paid for yours.

Another common question I am asked is regarding frequent flyer mileage. It is true that most courier flights will give you frequent flyer mileage; however, there are occasions when the courier company, in order to get a low fare from the airline, will waive the right to frequent flyer mileage for that particular airline. Usually, when companies do not offer you the frequent flyer mileage, the ticket tends to be even more discounted than other courier flights. Attempt to obtain the frequent flyer mileage by requesting it from the courier company, and the airline even after the flight, if necessary.

Nobody will know that you are an air courier unless you tell them, and do tell them. It is a great conversation piece and gives you an added mystique. Usually when I travel, I strike up a conversation with someone in the airport and tell them I am traveling as a courier. Before I know it, I have got a crowd of twenty people surrounding me. But most important, be sure to tell them about this book so they too can save on airfare!

WHAT ARE THE ADVANTAGES OF COURIER TRAVEL?

What is that saying, "You don't get something for nothing"? Well, in the case of courier travel, this is only partially true. While you do have the opportunity to save on airfares to nearly every major city around the world, there is a "price" to pay. But first let's look at the positive aspects.

The money you save is the greatest advantage to courier travel. How else can you fly from New York to Singapore for $150 roundtrip, or Los Angeles to London for $199? The money you save should more than compensate for any inconveniences that may arise. For those of you on a limited budget and who had planned on traveling light, this is a "win-win" situation.

There are no advance purchase penalties. When dealing with an airline directly, you often have to pay a hefty price for tickets not purchased seven, fourteen, or even twenty-one days in advance—a long time for you "spur of the moment" types. As an air courier, you will not be penalized for making travel arrangements only a few days in advance. In fact, your willingness to travel on the spur of the moment can be your leverage with the courier company. If the company needs to sell a ticket fast, you will probably be able to purchase the seat for very little or even free. For example, I recently found a courier flight from Los Angeles to Hong Kong for $150 roundtrip—provided I was willing to leave within three days. When I called the airline, I discovered that a ticket on that same flight and on that same date would cost over $1,500 if purchased through the "normal" route! That is ten times more than the cost of the courier flight. You do not have to be a brain surgeon to figure out what a terrific deal courier travel can be.

Finally, courier travel is fun. You will be exposed to a whole new industry and way of travel. When you meet another courier in the airport, you will have much to talk about—cities visited, courier companies used, and so forth. So when you meet that other courier in the airport, sit down, have a drink, and get to know your new friend.

ARE THERE DISADVANTAGES?

There are a few limitations to courier travel; however, they are heavily outweighed by its advantages. The disadvantages begin with the fact that you will sometimes not be allowed to bring all of your luggage to be checked in (as the whole basis behind courier travel is that you give up some or all of your luggage space in return for a discounted ticket). Although this does not mean you must travel empty-handed. Most couriers are very creative people. (If they were not, they would be paying hundreds of dollars more for the same flight!) Use your creativity to get around this problem.

Even though you might not be able to check in luggage, you always will be allowed to bring one or two carry-on bags. The airlines usually do not bother you provided that you do not attempt to bring on a huge suitcase that you intend to fit under your seat. The airlines' flexibility with this rule is dependent on how full the flight is. Two full bags should be more than enough clothing to cover a week or two in a foreign city. Most people over-pack. I have yet to meet anybody who does not take too much, including myself. Traveling lightly is an advantage because it gives you greater mobility.

In the event you need more room, there is something else you can do. Though the airline will only allow two bags to be carried on, there is no restriction on the amount of clothing you can wear on the plane. I am very serious about this. If you need a heavy coat where you are going, wear it on the plane. Do the same for a heavy sweater, shirts, and so on.

You can always bring in your pocket a rolled-up nylon bag. Once on the plane, start shedding some of your clothing. The airline only restricts you on the number of bags that you can bring on the plane. If you board with two bags and disembark with three, consider yourself creative.

Another disadvantage to courier travel is the small hassle before and after your flight. Air courier companies usually require you to be at the airport one to three hours before the plane departs, depending on the destination. I actually enjoy this time because it has given me the opportunity to meet and talk with other couriers. Upon arrival you will also need to meet with a courier representative. Try not to let this small inconvenience sway you, though. It is small in comparison to the savings involved.

HOW DO I BOOK A FLIGHT?

To book a flight, all you need is the information listed in this book. You do not need to be a member of any organization or association to be a courier. Be wary of those people who tell you otherwise. If you have any questions regarding this, feel free to write to me in care of the publisher.

While you need not be a member of any association, some courier companies charge you a minimal registration fee. For example, Now Voyager charges a $50 per year annual fee. This is noted in the courier company directory. My recommendation is to seek out courier companies first which do not have such a charge. Over the past couple of years, many of these charges have been eliminated.

Once you have decided on your destination, it is time to contact a courier company. You can skim through the directory of worldwide courier destinations to help you locate a city in which courier flights are available. The index in the back of this book will help you cross-reference destinations and departure cities. It is important to note that the cities to which companies offer courier flights are constantly changing. Once you have contacted the courier company, it will help you locate a date and a location that is available to them and acceptable to you.

If your goal is to take more than one courier flight on one trip, it is possible to arrange this through one company. Jupiter Air can do this. For example, if you want to fly from San Francisco to Singapore and then continue from Singapore to Bangkok, all of this can be arranged with one phone call. Or if you want to travel from Los Angeles to London and then from London to Tokyo, this is also possible by making only one phone call.

Another often asked question is, "how far in advance must a courier flight be booked?" Ideally, courier companies like to fill their schedules two to three months in advance. As an example of a two month schedule, beginning on October 1, the courier companies will take reservations for flights through December. Therefore, it is a good idea to contact companies on the first of the month, because that is when they open up their schedules. However, the best deals can be found if you are willing to travel on short notice.

At times, getting in contact with some courier companies is easier said than done. The phone lines at Now Voyager and Halbart Express are often tied up with other budget-minded travelers like yourself, and it may require a great deal of patience to get through. Some courier companies, such as World Courier, require you to call and leave your name and address, and they will mail you an application. This tends to be quite burdensome and is one reason why I have not flown with this company. Don't let these inconveniences deter you; it is still worth it. However, the majority of courier company offices are extremely friendly. They will assist you in getting you where you want to go for as inexpensively as possible. Some companies can offer you additional travel services, aside from the courier flights, such as non-courier flights.

Some courier companies, especially the larger ones, require you to call them a day before you make your reservation. These companies have extensive recorded messages detailing all the flights available, last minute bargains, length of stay, etc. This is important for these companies which offer so many courier flights, that it would take too long for them to explain everything to you. For example, one courier company offers over thirty roundtrip tickets between New York and London alone every week. They do not have the manpower to list all of these flights to callers personally. Some courier companies do not even handle the reservations themselves, opting instead to use courier brokers.

Not all courier companies are set up to book the flights, take reservations, handle payments, and deal with customers. This is where courier brokers fit in. The brokers essentially fill the seats for the courier companies. Courier brokers represent one or more courier companies. Therefore, they can provide you with numerous tickets on the same flight using different courier companies. However, nobody works for free. The courier broker usually adds a service fee to the price of the ticket. Generally, you will get a cheaper fare if you deal directly with the courier company. The advantage to courier brokers is they might represent many courier companies and have access to many more tickets or destinations. The directory will list whether the company is a broker or courier company.

After you make a reservation with a courier company—that is, after you initially call and choose a date and city—the company will send you a contract. Some companies require that you have the payment and the signed contract returned to them within a week. The generally accepted forms of payment will be discussed in the upcoming section. It is possible—and sometimes desirable—to have the courier company fax you a copy of the contract in order for you to get the payment to them more quickly and secure your reservation. Different courier companies have different requirements, formats, and policies.

It is important to keep track of your communications with the courier company, especially the name of the person you talked with. These people talk to many people each and every day and have a tendency to forget what was arranged with any particular person. Although the courier industry is quite large, the division of the courier company that schedules onboard couriers like yourself is usually quite small—often only one or two people. Additionally, when people call a courier company, they are expected to have a basic knowledge of courier travel. The courier company employees do not have the time to personally explain the basics of courier travel to every person that calls. This book does that for them.

How can I pay for a courier flight?

Courier companies often have different ways of collecting payment: some accept credit cards while others accept only money orders or certified checks. Others will accept personal checks provided they have the opportunity to clear the bank prior to the flight's departure. Some companies can accept cash payments at their offices. So if you live in or near New York, Los Angeles, San Francisco, Toronto, or other cities that have courier flights departing from them, it is possible to pay in cash at the courier company office. This could be the case if you are flying at the last minute and do not have time to mail a check. For example, if you find a flight departing New York to Paris for $99 roundtrip that leaves in two days, you will have to make your payment in person at the courier office. Be sure to discuss this with them.

Most courier companies do not charge a deposit on the flight, although some courier companies still do. This is to ensure you take the roundtrip. This is especially true if you have never taken a courier flight with this particular company before. They do this to protect themselves from the possibility of somebody not fulfilling their end of the bargain. Deposits range from $50 to $500. Some companies allow you to put this deposit on a credit card while others require it up front. In this case, your deposit will be refunded upon your return. Sometimes, once you have flown with a company, the deposit is waived.

The important thing to remember about courier travel is that money talks. Usually, the first person to pay for a flight gets it. When a courier company pencils you in for a flight, it gives you a certain amount of time to get the payment in. For example, the company might give you five days, after which it will cancel your reservation and make the flight available to somebody else. Keep in touch with them. If you think your payment will not be received in time, call them to let them know this. You do not want to lose your flight due to miscommunication.

How long can I stay?

Length of stay is another subject with a lot of variables. In some cases, the courier company sets the length of stay. In others, the company sets a range of dates for return and you get to choose the length of your stay. Stays can range from one week to one year. When you look through the courier company directory, the lengths of stay will be listed in most cases. Whether they are listed or not, this is something you should discuss with the courier company. Most courier companies will work with your schedule. You are doing the courier company a favor. Without you, they would not be in business.

It is also possible to return from different cities. For example, one could fly to Mexico City and return from other cities in Mexico, such as Cancun or Acapulco. I've done this myself. Again, this depends on which courier company you choose to fly with. Be sure to ask them about this as well.

Can I cancel or get a refund?

If you must cancel a courier flight, cancellation charges generally do apply. The cancellation policy will be outlined in their contract. However in most cases, the percentage of your payment held depends on the number of days prior to the flight that the cancellation is made. If you cancel at the last minute, or miss your flight, you will probably lose the full amount of your fare. This policy is very similar to buying a non-refundable ticket on a commercial airline.

Refunds are usually not available; however, in certain cases I have heard of people receiving some refunds. This has to do with how far in advance they made their reservation and how far in advance they canceled their flight. Remember, the courier company must fill that seat on a certain day. When you see flights offered for free, they are sometimes the result of someone else's last-minute cancellation.

CAN I TRAVEL WITH A COMPANION?

Absolutely. While courier travel is extremely popular with the independent traveler, there are many opportunities for travel with a companion. While independent travel is enjoyable, and I have done a lot of it in my time, I prefer to share my international experiences with a partner. In my courier trips, I usually travel with my wife. While simple, courier travel with a companion does require some additional planning.

The basis of courier travel is to give up some or all of your luggage space in exchange for subsidized airfare. Therefore, a courier company might only need one seat on a particular flight. So if this is the case, how does your travel partner get there with you?

One method is to attempt to arrange for both of you to travel on the same flight with the same courier company. This is possible because some companies do send numerous couriers on the same flight. There are times when more than one courier is needed for heavy shipments. Courier brokers can assist you in getting two people on the same flight. This might be done through two different courier companies using the same broker. This is ideal because it only requires one phone call, and there is only one check to write.

Another possibility is for both of you to travel with the same courier company and on the same day, although on different flights. Some city combinations, such as from New York to London, are so popular that there is more than one courier flight per day. If you travel on different flights, then the first traveler may utilize the extra time by making arrangements for lodging.

One of the most common ways people travel together as couriers is for one person to travel one day and the other to fly the very next day. Remember that these companies purchase tickets for the same flight each and every day. For example, on a recent two-week courier trip to London, I flew on Tuesday and my wife flew on the same flight to London that Wednesday. When I originally tried to book our reservations, I asked for two consecutive days, preferably a Monday and Tuesday. Unfortunately, that Monday was already booked, so we took the Tuesday and Wednesday courier flights. Flexibility is paramount with courier travel. This is how you will save the greatest amount of money.

Upon my arrival, I used the extra day to locate an inexpensive place to stay in London—not an easy task, I might say. Check the resource section in this book for a list of budget accommodations in major courier cities. Whatever slight inconvenience I encountered, it was more than made up for by the money we saved. Additionally, the courier company allowed my wife and me to switch the return dates in order for my wife to return to the States the day before I did. Most courier companies will attempt to work with you. If you have a specific travel request, be sure to ask the courier company.

Flying to different cities and then meeting later is another possibility for people traveling together. For example, one person could fly to Singapore and the other to Bangkok. Or, one person could fly to Madrid and the other to Lisbon. Transportation between the cities is relatively inexpensive. This is usually very easy to arrange, because most courier companies offer flights to major cities each and every day.

Yet another option is for one person to fly using a commercial ticket on the same flight as the courier. Although one ticket will cost substantially more, the two of you can split the cost and you will still be flying for less than anyone else on that airplane. For example, you could buy a ticket through a courier company to Hong Kong for $200 roundtrip. Your travel partner could buy a ticket on the same flight for $800 roundtrip through a travel agent. The total cost to both of you would be $1,000 or $500 each, far less than any other way to Hong Kong, except perhaps by the proverbial slow boat to China. The choice is yours.

Although you must be at least eighteen to fly as a courier, it is still possible to travel with children. Many courier companies allow you to bring a child without any additional charge. There are usually some restrictions. For instance, one company might allow you to bring a child provided they are over the age of two, while another company might have a different requirement. One thing is for sure, you will not be allowed to take any nineteen-year-old children with you for free. An additional restriction will be based on the airline's rules regarding children. For example, some airlines allow children to fly for free only up until the age of two, whereas other airlines might have different policies.

WHAT ARE MY RESPONSIBILITIES AS A COURIER?

Your most important responsibility is to follow the requirements designated by the courier company. These requirements will be outlined in your contract, which you usually must sign. Some courier companies also have a "Terms and Conditions" sheet, which they will make you aware of.

First and foremost, you are not an employee of the courier company. You are an independent contractor. You are not on their payroll, they will not pay your health insurance, and you will not receive a pension. What you will receive is a deeply discounted airline ticket.

However, you will be representing the courier company both to the public and to the airline, even if nobody knows you are a courier. You can be sure that if you get drunk on your flight and are arrested, the courier company will hear about it. Do not jeopardize courier travel for the rest of us. You have a responsibility to your fellow travelers to not destroy this tradition.

Different courier companies have different expectations of your conduct. Some courier companies will not allow you to drink alcohol; others will. That does not mean if you are flying as a courier on British Airways, which offers complimentary alcoholic beverages, that you should finish off every drink on the plane. The bottom line is: know your limits.

THE DAY OF THE FLIGHT

The day of the flight you will need to meet an agent from the courier company at a place designated by the company. This can be at any one of a number of locations, including a specific spot at the airport terminal or at the courier company office, usually located on the grounds of the airport. The airport terminal is the most common location.

The courier company will usually require you to be at the airport a minimum of two hours prior to the flight in order for them to check your passport, check in any luggage you might have, give you a copy of the manifest and check you in for the flight. Additionally, the agent you meet prior to flight will give you a printed copy of instructions, which includes your return flight information and where to meet the courier agent when you arrive. Usually, this process does not take long. The courier representatives are very helpful—remember, you are actually doing them a great favor. Without you, they would not be in business.

You will not be required to do any lifting, lugging, carrying, tugging, dragging, pushing, pulling, or hauling of any material for a courier company. You are essentially just going along for the ride. The courier company delivers the material to the airline and picks it up upon arrival. Your job is merely to show the manifest to the customs officer when you reach your destination.

Courier companies have different requirements concerning dress. Many require you to dress professionally whereas others will let you fly in shorts. This is another question you need to discuss with the courier company. You should not have any problems if your appearance is not in the extreme.

Yet another responsibility has to do with flight confirmation. Often you need to call the courier company to confirm your flight schedule. This is done to ensure that you know when you are traveling. They might ask you to confirm this on both the departure and return flights.

You will need a valid passport, which will enable entry to and exit from your courier destination. Furthermore, you might need a visa, depending on where you are traveling to. You are responsible for all your own lodging and all your other expenses when you reach your destination. Some flights do include stopovers in various cities, and in these cases the courier companies will pay for your night's lodging in these cities.

Now you have the information you need to travel inexpensively and enjoy many exciting destinations. The following page includes a list of courier tips to ensure your trip goes as smoothly as possible. The resource section will assist you with lodging and travel information. I hope courier travel brings you as much enjoyment as it has for me over the years. Good luck and happy travels!

COURIER TIPS

✈ Be aware of the basics of supply and demand. Seek out off-season travel for the best savings.

✈ Call courier companies at the beginning of the month for the best selection of available flights.

✈ Ensure that you have a visa if one is required, and keep your passport up to date.

✈ Carry *The Courier Air Travel Handbook* with you when you travel, which details the phone numbers of worldwide courier companies for easy reference.

✈ Join the frequent flyer program of the airline.

✈ When meeting the courier company, be sure you have change with you for a phone call in case they are late or you are in the wrong place.

✈ Pack lightly. Just about everybody over-packs. The less stuff you have, the more mobile you will be.

✈ Try to plan ahead and have an idea of where you will stay the first night.

✈ Keep your passport, return ticket, courier information, and traveler's checks in a safe place. Losing one of these items can be painful.

✈ Remember that each courier company has its own set of policies, and you must follow their procedures exactly.

PART II

COURIER

COMPANY DIRECTORY

The following pages list active courier companies. Please note the proper times to call; this will save you time and money. Although phone numbers do change, at the time of printing, all numbers were current. Every attempt has been made to locate toll-free numbers; however, these numbers are often closely guarded secrets.

The directory is organized by geographic region and then by country. Courier companies are listed alphabetically under the cities in which their flights originate.

COURIER DIRECTORY CONTENTS

EUROPE

At the time this book was being printed, Bridges Worldwide changed its name to Virgin Express for its North American operations.

NORTH AMERICA

COURIER COMPANY LISTINGS

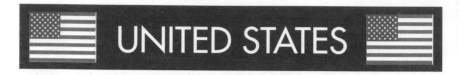

UNITED STATES

CHICAGO

Halbart Express

Destination	R/T fare	Last-minute fare	Length of stay/Departure days
London	**$450**	**$300**	**Up to 2 months Wed–Mon**

Flights originating from: Chicago
Address: 1475 Elmhurst
City/State/Zip: Grove Village, IL 60009
Phone: 847-806-1250
Toll-free number: No
Point of contact: Julie
Times to call: 11AM–5PM CST Mon–Fri
Recorded information: No
Type of business: Courier company
Conducting business since: 1983
Annual registration fee: No
Courier assignment length: Up to 60 days
Luggage restrictions: Carry-on only
Frequent flyer mileage accrued: Yes
Airlines used: American
Return date flexibility: No
One-way tickets available: No
Cancellation phone list: No
Last-minute discounts: Yes
Additional non-courier travel services: Yes
Recommended advance reservations: Four–six weeks
Earliest possible reservations: Three months
Departure taxes: $28.50
Deposit: No
Method of payment: Cash, money order, cashier's check
Credit cards accepted: No
Comments: The staff are very friendly and helpful.

Jupiter/Micom America

Destination	R/T fare	Last-minute fare	Length of stay/Departure days
London	$250	Varies	1–2 weeks Tue–Sat
Hong Kong	$450	Varies	9–30 days Tue–Sun

Flights originating from: Chicago
Address: 224 Howard Avenue
City/State/Zip: Des Plains, IL 60018
Phone: 708-298-3850
Fax: 708-298-3854
Toll-free number: No
Point of contact: Anyone
Times to call: 9AM–5PM CST Mon–Fri
Recorded information: No
Type of business: Courier company
Conducting business since: 1988
Annual registration fee: $35
Courier assignment length: Seven–thirty days
Luggage restrictions: London: One carry-on and one checked bag; Hong Kong: Carry-on only
Frequent flyer mileage accrued: Yes
Airlines used: United, Japan Air
Return date flexibility: No
One-way tickets available: Yes
Cancellation phone list: Yes
Last-minute discounts: Yes
Additional non-courier travel services: Yes
Recommended advance reservations: One month
Earliest possible reservations: One month
Departure taxes: No
Deposit: $100
Method of payment: Personal check
Credit cards accepted: No
Comments: If you want to ensure a return date that works with your schedule, you should call one month before departure.

HOUSTON

Now Voyager

Destination	R/T fare	Last-minute fare	Length of stay/Departure days
London	**$299**	**$99**	**Up to 30 days Mon–Fri**

Flights originating from: Houston
Address: 74 Varick Street, Room 307
City/State/Zip: New York, NY 10013
Phone: 212-431-1616
Fax: 212-334-5243
Toll-free number: No
Point of contact: Anyone
Times to call: 10AM–5:30PM EST Sat
Recorded information: 11PM–5:30PM EST Mon–Fri
Type of business: Courier broker
Conducting business since: 1983
Annual registration fee: $50
Courier assignment length: Up to 30 days; one week is the usual length
Luggage restrictions: Carry-on only
Frequent flyer mileage accrued: Yes
Airlines used: Continental
Return date flexibility: Yes
One-way tickets available: Yes
Cancellation phone list: Yes (Jet-setter program)
Last-minute discounts: Yes—one of the best selections in the industry
Additional non-courier travel services: Non-courier discount domestic flights
Recommended advance reservations: Two months
Earliest possible reservations: Three months
Departure taxes: No
Deposit: $100 for most flights
Method of payment: Cash, money order, cashier's check, personal check, traveler's check
Credit cards accepted: Yes
Comments: This is an extremely busy company and it is usually difficult to get through on the phone. They offer one of the largest selection of courier flights in the world. Most flights originate in New York. Be sure to call the information line prior to talking with an agent. Prices are slightly higher during summer months. It is possible to obtain a Houston to London flight for $175 R/T.

LOS ANGELES

Virgin Express

Destination	R/T fare	Last-minute fare	Length of stay/Departure days
London	**$400–$450**	**No**	**Up to 6 weeks**

Flights originating from: Los Angeles
Address: Building 197, JFK International Airport
City/State/Zip: Jamaica, NY 11430
Phone: 718-244-7244
Fax: 718-244-7240
Toll-free number: No
Point of contact: Anyone
Times to call: 9AM–5PM EST Mon–Fri
Recorded information: No
Type of business: Courier broker
Conducting business since: 1991
Annual registration fee: No
Courier assignment length: Up to six weeks
Luggage restrictions: Carry-on and two pieces of luggage
Frequent flyer mileage accrued: Yes
Airlines used: Virgin
Return date flexibility: No
One-way tickets available: No
Cancellation phone list: No
Last-minute discounts: No
Additional non-courier travel services: No
Recommended advance reservations: Two months
Earliest possible reservations: Two months
Departure taxes: Included in price
Deposit: No
Method of payment: Cash or personal check
Credit cards accepted: Yes

East West Express

Destination	R/T fare	Last-minute fare	Length of stay/Departure days
Sydney	**$1,050**	**No**	**Up to 90 days daily**
Melbourne	**$1,050**	**No**	**Up to 30 days daily**

Flights originating from: Los Angeles
Address: P.O. Box 30849, JFK Airport Station
City/State/Zip: Jamaica, NY 11430
Phone: 718-656-6246
Toll-free number: No
Point of contact: Tracy
Times to call: 9AM–5PM EST
Recorded information: No
Type of business: Courier broker
Conducting business since: 1991
Annual registration fee: No
Courier assignment length: Up to 90 days
Luggage restrictions: Carry-on only on the outgoing flight. You can check luggage on the return flight.
Frequent flyer mileage accrued: No
Airlines used: Qantas
Return date flexibility: Yes
One-way tickets available: No
Cancellation phone list: No
Last-minute discounts: No
Additional non-courier travel services: No
Recommended advance reservations: Two months
Earliest possible reservations: Two months
Departure taxes: No
Deposit: No
Method of payment: Cash or cashier's check
Credit cards accepted: No
Comments: This company is friendly and helpful. The Australia trips are popular, so you will definitely need to book in advance.

Film Freight International

Destination	R/T fare	Last-minute fare	Length of stay/Departure days
Mexico City	**$250–$275**	**Varies**	**Up to 1 month Mon–Thu, Sat**

Flights originating from: Los Angeles
Address: 8900 Bellance Avenue
City/State/Zip: Los Angeles, CA 90045
Phone: 310-568-8403
Toll-free number: No
Point of contact: Milton
Times to call: 9AM–5PM PST
Recorded information: No
Type of business: Courier broker
Conducting business since: 1984
Annual registration fee: No
Courier assignment length: Up to one month
Luggage restrictions: Carry-on or else $31 for luggage
Frequent flyer mileage accrued: Yes
Airlines used: Lacsa
Return date flexibility: Yes
One-way tickets available: No
Cancellation phone list: Yes
Last-minute discounts: Yes
Additional non-courier travel services: No
Recommended advance reservations: One month
Earliest possible reservations: One month
Departure taxes: No
Deposit: $100 non-refundable
Method of payment: Cash or personal check
Credit cards accepted: No

Halbart Express

Destination	R/T fare	Last-minute fare	Length of stay/Departure days
Sydney	**$750**	**No**	**2 weeks Tue, Wed, Sat**

Flights originating from: Los Angeles
Address: 14705 176th Street
City/State/Zip: Jamaica, NY 11434
Phone: 718-656-8189
Fax: 718-244-0559
Toll-free number: No
Point of contact: Anyone
Times to call: 9AM–3PM EST Mon–Fri
Recorded information: Yes
Type of business: Courier company
Conducting business since: 1983
Annual registration fee: $50 for first-time flyers
Courier assignment length: Two weeks
Luggage restrictions: Carry-on only
Frequent flyer mileage accrued: Yes
Airlines used: Air New Zealand
Return date flexibility: No
One-way tickets available: No
Cancellation phone list: No
Last-minute discounts: No
Additional non-courier travel services: No
Recommended advance reservations: Two–three months
Earliest possible reservations: Two–three months
Departure taxes: No
Deposit: No
Method of payment: Certified checks, money order, cash
Credit cards accepted: No
Comments: This flight fills up fast. You'll need to call a couple of months in advance.

International Bonded Couriers (IBC)

Destination	R/T fare	Last-minute fare	Length of stay/Departure days
Bangkok	**$450**	**$200**	**2 weeks Mon–Fri**
Hong Kong	**$350**	**$150**	**2 weeks Tue–Sat**
Manila	**$350**	**$250**	**2 weeks, 4 flights per week Tue–Sat**
Singapore	**$350**	**$150**	**Up to 2 months Tue–Sat**
Taipei	**$350**	**$250**	**9–15 days, overnight in Seoul Tue–Sat**
Tokyo	**$450**	**$100**	**9 days Tue–Sat**

Flights originating from: Los Angeles
Address: 1595 E El Segundo Boulevard
City/State/Zip: El Segundo, CA 90245
Phone: 310-607-0125
Fax: 310-607-0126
Toll-free number: No
Point of contact: Jo
Times to call: 9AM–4PM PST Tue–Fri
Recorded information: No
Type of business: Courier company
Conducting business since: 1988
Annual registration fee: No
Courier assignment length: Two weeks–six months
Luggage restrictions: No restrictions
Frequent flyer mileage accrued: Yes
Airlines used: Northwest
Return date flexibility: No restrictions
One-way tickets available: Yes
Cancellation phone list: Yes
Last-minute discounts: No
Additional non-courier travel services: Yes
Recommended advance reservations: One month
Earliest possible reservations: Six months
Departure taxes: No
Deposit: $500
Method of payment: Certified check, money order, cash, personal check
Credit cards accepted: Yes
Comments: Prices usually remain the same throughout the year.

Jupiter Air

Destination	R/T fare	Last-minute fare	Length of stay/Departure days
Sydney	**$650**	**Varies**	**1–2 weeks**

Flights originating from: Los Angeles
Address: 460 Hindry Avenue, Unit D
City/State/Zip: Inglewood, CA 90301
Phone: 310-670-5123
Fax: 310-649-2771
Toll-free number: No
Point of contact: Levine or Sarah
Times to call: 9AM–5:30PM PST Mon–Fri
Recorded information: No
Type of business: Courier company
Conducting business since: 1988
Annual registration fee: $35
Courier assignment length: One–two weeks
Luggage restrictions: Carry-on only to Singapore; one bag to Hong Kong and Seoul
Frequent flyer mileage accrued: No
Airlines used: JAL, Singapore, Asiana
Return date flexibility: No
One-way tickets available: No
Cancellation phone list: Yes
Last-minute discounts: Yes
Additional non-courier travel services: No
Recommended advance reservations: Two months
Earliest possible reservations: Three months
Departure taxes: No
Deposit: $100
Method of payment: Certified check, money order, cash, personal check
Credit cards accepted: No
Comments: Prices are slightly higher during summer months.

Midnight Express

Destination	R/T fare	Last-minute fare	Length of stay/Departure days
London	**$350**	**$200**	**2 weeks Sat**

Flights originating from: Los Angeles
Address: 930 W Hyde Park Boulevard
City/State/Zip: Inglewood, CA 90302
Phone: 310-672-1100
Fax: 310-671-0107
Toll-free number: No
Point of contact: Tammy
Times to call: 12PM–3PM PST Mon–Fri
Recorded information: No
Type of business: Courier company
Conducting business since: 1988
Annual registration fee: No
Courier assignment length: Two weeks–six months
Luggage restrictions: Carry-on only on the outgoing flight. You can check luggage on the return flight.
Frequent flyer mileage accrued: Yes
Airlines used: United
Return date flexibility: No restrictions
One-way tickets available: Yes
Cancellation phone list: Yes
Last-minute discounts: No
Additional non-courier travel services: Yes
Recommended advance reservations: One month
Earliest possible reservations: Six months
Departure taxes: No
Deposit: $500
Method of payment: Certified check, money order, cash, personal check
Credit cards accepted: No
Comments: You must live in Southern California to fly as a courier with this company.

Now Voyager

Destination	R/T fare	Last-minute fare	Length of stay/Departure days
Sydney	**$699–$1,199**	**Varies**	**Up to 3 months**

Flights originating from: Los Angeles
Address: 74 Varick Street, Suite 307
City/State/Zip: New York, NY 10013
Phone: 212-431-1616
Fax: 212-219-1753 or 212-334-5243
Toll-free number: No
Point of contact: Anyone
Times to call: 10AM–5:30PM EST Mon–Fri
Recorded information: 11:00AM–5:30PM EST Mon–Fri
Type of business: Courier broker
Conducting business since: 1983
Annual registration fee: $50
Courier assignment length: Up to three months
Luggage restrictions: Carry-on only
Frequent flyer mileage accrued: Yes
Airlines used: Qantas, Air New Zealand
Return date flexibility: No
One-way tickets available: No
Cancellation phone list: Yes
Last-minute discounts: Yes
Additional non-courier travel services: Yes
Recommended advance reservations: Two–three months
Earliest possible reservations: Two–three months
Departure taxes: No
Deposit: $100
Method of payment: Money order, cash, cashier's check
Credit cards accepted: Yes
Comments: This is a busy company and it is difficult to get through by phone. First-time flyers should listen to the recording.

MIAMI

East West Express

Destination	R/T fare	Last-minute fare	Length of stay/Departure days
Sydney	**$1,050**	**$1,250**	**Up to 90 days Tue–Sat**
Melbourne	**$1,050**	**$1,250**	**Up to 90 days Tue–Sat**

Flights originating from: Miami
Address: P.O. Box 30849, JFK Airport Station
City/State/Zip: Jamaica, NY 11430
Phone: 718-656-6246
Toll-free number: No
Point of contact: Tracy
Times to call: 9AM–5PM EST
Recorded information: No
Type of business: Courier broker
Conducting business since: 1991
Annual registration fee: No
Courier assignment length: Up to 90 days
Luggage restrictions: Carry-on only on the outgoing flight. You can check luggage on the return flight.
Frequent flyer mileage accrued: No
Airlines used: Qantas
Return date flexibility: Yes
One-way tickets available: No
Cancellation phone list: No
Last-minute discounts: No
Additional non-courier travel services: No
Recommended advance reservations: Two months
Earliest possible reservations: Two months
Departure taxes: No
Deposit: No
Method of payment: Cash or cashier's check
Credit cards accepted: No
Comments: This company is friendly and helpful. The Australia trips are popular, so you will definitely need to book in advance.

Film Freight International

Destination	R/T fare	Last-minute fare	Length of stay/Departure days
Mexico City	**$250**	**Varies**	**Up to 1 month Mon–Thu, Sat**

Flights originating from: Miami
Address: 8900 Bellance Avenue
City/State/Zip: Los Angeles, CA 90045
Phone: 310-568-8403
Toll-free number: No
Point of contact: Milton
Times to call: 9AM–5PM PST
Recorded information: No
Type of business: Courier broker
Conducting business since: 1984
Annual registration fee: No
Courier assignment length: Up to one month
Luggage restrictions: Carry-on only
Frequent flyer mileage accrued: Yes
Airlines used: Lacsa
Return date flexibility: Yes
One-way tickets available: No
Cancellation phone list: Yes
Last-minute discounts: Yes
Additional non-courier travel services: No
Recommended advance reservations: One month
Earliest possible reservations: One month
Departure taxes: No
Deposit: $100 non-refundable
Method of payment: Cash or personal check
Credit cards accepted: No

Halbart Express

Destination	R/T fare	Last-minute fare	Length of stay/Departure days
Sao Paulo	**$400**	**Varies**	**1 week Mon–Sat**

Flights originating from: Miami
Address: 2471 NW 72nd Avenue
City/State/Zip: Miami, FL 33122
Phone: 305-593-0260
Fax: 305-593-0158
Toll-free number: No
Point of contact: Stella Tome or Antonio Cano
Times to call: 9AM–5PM EST Mon–Fri
Recorded information: No
Type of business: Courier company
Conducting business since: 1983
Annual registration fee: No
Courier assignment length: One–two weeks
Luggage restrictions: Carry-on only
Frequent flyer mileage accrued: Yes
Airlines used: American, Iberia, LanChile
Return date flexibility: No
One-way tickets available: Yes, sometimes
Cancellation phone list: Yes
Last-minute discounts: Yes
Additional non-courier travel services: No
Recommended advance reservations: Two months
Earliest possible reservations: Two months
Departure taxes: $28, already included in price
Deposit: No
Method of payment: Certified check, money order, cash
Credit cards accepted: No
Comments: Prices are slightly higher during summer months. The Miami office of Halbart is extremely friendly and helpful. I highly recommend this company for courier flights. They offer good opportunities for heavily discounted, and sometimes free, flights. On one day in August 1993, Halbart gave a round-trip ticket to Santiago for free, one to Buenos Aires for $178, and one to Caracas for $99!

International Bonded Couriers (IBC)

Destination	R/T fare	Last-minute fare	Length of stay/Departure days
Buenos Aires	**$400**	**Varies**	**1–2 weeks Mon, Thu, Sat**

Flights originating from: Miami
Address: 8401 NW 17th Street
City/State/Zip: Miami, FL 33126
Phone: 305-591-8080
Fax: 305-591-2056
Toll-free number: No
Point of contact: Ernesto
Times to call: 10AM–5PM EST
Recorded information: No
Type of business: Courier broker
Conducting business since: 1981
Annual registration fee: No
Courier assignment length: One–two weeks
Luggage restrictions: Carry-on only
Frequent flyer mileage accrued: Yes
Airlines used: Ladeco
Return date flexibility: No
One-way tickets available: No
Cancellation phone list: No
Last-minute discounts: Yes
Additional non-courier travel services: No
Recommended advance reservations: Two–three months
Earliest possible reservations: Two–three months
Departure taxes: No
Deposit: No
Method of payment: Money order, cashier's check
Credit cards accepted: Yes

International Business Couriers

Destination	R/T fare	Last-minute fare	Length of stay/Departure days
Port of Spain, Trinidad	**$100**	**No**	**1 week to 1 month Mon–Thu, Sat**

Flights originating from: Miami
Address: 102 SE Vincent Street
City/State/Zip: Port of Spain, Trinidad
Phone: 809-623-4231
Toll-free number: No
Point of contact: Lisa Ramsaran
Times to call: 8:15AM–4PM EST
Recorded information: No
Type of business: Courier broker
Annual registration fee: No
Courier assignment length: One week–one month
Luggage restrictions: Carry-on only
Frequent flyer mileage accrued: Yes
Airlines used: WIA
Return date flexibility: No
One-way tickets available: No
Cancellation phone list: No
Last-minute discounts: No
Additional non-courier travel services: No
Recommended advance reservations: Two months
Earliest possible reservations: Two months
Departure taxes: No
Deposit: No
Method of payment: Cash or traveler's check
Credit cards accepted: No
Comments: This company is friendly, accommodating to travelers' schedules, and easy to work with.

Linehaul Services

Destination	R/T fare	Last-minute fare	Length of stay/Departure days
Madrid	$375	$200	1 week
Buenos Aires	$475	$250	Up to 21 days Mon–Thu, Sat
Caracas	$173	$100	Up to 3 weeks Mon–Thu, Sat
Guatemala City	$223	$150	Up to 1 year Sun–Thu
Guayaquil	$225	$150	Up to 3 weeks Mon–Thu, Sat
La Paz	$425	$150	Up to 3 weeks Mon–Thu, Sat
Quito	$250	$150	Up to 3 weeks Mon–Thu, Sat
Rio de Janeiro	$475	$250	Up to 3 weeks Mon–Thu, Sat
Sao Paulo	$475	$250	1 to 3 weeks Mon–Thu, Sat

Flights originating from: Miami
Address: 7859 NW 15th Street
City/State/Zip: Miami, FL 33126
Phone: 305-477-0651
Fax: 305-477-0659
Toll-free number: No
Point of contact: Ileana
Times to call: 9AM–5:30PM Mon–Fri; 10:30AM–1:30PM Sat EST
Recorded information: No
Type of business: Courier company
Conducting business since: 1985
Annual registration fee: No
Courier assignment length: One week–one year
Luggage restrictions: Carry-on only
Frequent flyer mileage accrued: Yes
Airlines used: American, Varig, Argentina
Return date flexibility: Yes
One-way tickets available: Yes
Cancellation phone list: Yes
Last-minute discounts: Yes
Additional non-courier travel services: No
Recommended advance reservations: One month
Earliest possible reservations: Two months
Departure taxes: Included in price
Deposit: No
Method of payment: Money order, cash
Credit cards accepted: No
Comments: Prices are slightly higher during summer months. This company is very helpful. They speak Spanish.

Trans-Air System

Destination	R/T fare	Last-minute fare	Length of stay/Departure days
Buenos Aires	**$460**	**$250**	**4-day minimum, 20-day maximum Mon–Thu, Sat**
Guatemala City	**$230**	**$150**	**Up to 1 year Mon–Fri**
Quito	**$250**	**$150**	**3 weeks Mon–Thu**
Santiago	**$460**	**$250**	**4-day minimum, 30-day maximum Mon–Thu, Sat**

Flights originating from: Miami
Address: 7264 NW 25th Street
City/State/Zip: Miami, FL 33122
Phone: 305-592-1771
Fax: 305-592-2927
Toll-free number: No
Point of contact: Ydania or Marisol
Times to call: 9:30AM–5:30PM EST Mon–Fri
Recorded information: No
Type of business: Courier company
Conducting business since: 1988
Annual registration fee: No
Courier assignment length: One week–one year
Luggage restrictions: Carry-on only
Frequent flyer mileage accrued: Yes
Airlines used: American
Return date flexibility: Yes
One-way tickets available: Yes
Cancellation phone list: Yes
Last-minute discounts: Yes
Additional non-courier travel services: No
Recommended advance reservations: One month
Earliest possible reservations: Two months
Departure taxes: $28
Deposit: $50
Method of payment: Money order, cash
Credit cards accepted: No
Comments: Prices are slightly higher during summer months. This company is very helpful. They speak Spanish.

NEW YORK

Air Facility

Destination	R/T fare	Last-minute fare	Length of stay/Departure days
Caracas	**$210**	**$100**	**6–7 days Tue–Fri, Sat**
Madrid	**$350**	**$180**	**Varies**
Mexico City	**$200**	**$100**	**Varies**
Rio de Janiero	**$480**	**$300**	**8, 9, or 14 days Tue, Wed, Sat**
Sao Paulo	**$340**	**$180**	**Varies**

Flights originating from: New York
Address: 153-40 Rockaway Boulevard
City/State/Zip: Jamaica, NY 11434
Phone: 718-712-1769
Fax: 718-712-1574
Toll-free number: No
Point of contact: Claudio, Ruth, or Alex
Times to call: 11AM–5PM EST Mon–Fri
Recorded information: No
Type of business: Courier company
Conducting business since: 1988
Annual registration fee: No
Courier assignment length: One–two weeks
Luggage restrictions: Carry-on only
Frequent flyer mileage accrued: No
Airlines used: Varig, LanChile, United, Ladeco
Return date flexibility: No
One-way tickets available: No
Cancellation phone list: Yes
Last-minute discounts: Yes
Additional non-courier travel services: No
Recommended advance reservations: One month
Earliest possible reservations: Three months
Departure taxes: $28
Deposit: No
Method of payment: Certified check, money order, cash, personal check
Credit cards accepted: No
Comments: Prices are slightly higher during summer months. Air Facility depends on responsible people to act as couriers for them. If you cancel a flight last minute, they place you on a black list, and you will not be allowed to fly with them in the future. They are helpful and offer consistently inexpensive fares to South America.

Virgin Express

Destination	R/T fare	Last-minute fare	Length of stay/Departure days
London	**$300–$360**	**No**	**Up to 6 weeks twice daily**

Flights originating from: New York
Address: Building 197, JFK International Airport
City/State/Zip: Jamaica, NY 11430
Phone: 718-244-7244
Fax: 718-244-7240
Toll-free number: No
Point of contact: Anyone
Times to call: 9AM–5PM EST Mon–Fri
Recorded information: No
Type of business: Courier broker
Conducting business since: 1991
Annual registration fee: No
Courier assignment length: Up to six weeks
Luggage restrictions: Carry-on and two pieces of luggage
Frequent flyer mileage accrued: Yes
Airlines used: Virgin
Return date flexibility: Yes
One-way tickets available: No
Cancellation phone list: No
Last-minute discounts: No
Additional non-courier travel services: No
Recommended advance reservations: Two months
Earliest possible reservations: Two months
Departure taxes: Included in price
Deposit: No
Method of payment: Cash or check
Credit cards accepted: Yes

Courier Network

Destination	R/T fare	Last-minute fare	Length of stay/Departure days
Tel Aviv	**$500**	**$500**	**1 week Mon–Thu, Sat**

Flights originating from: New York
Address: 295 7th Avenue
City/State/Zip: New York, NY 10001
Phone: 212-691-9860
Fax: 212-929-5186
Toll-free number: 800-222-9951
Point of contact: Anyone
Times to call: 6:30PM–9PM EST
Recorded information: No
Type of business: Courier broker
Conducting business since: 1987
Annual registration fee: No
Courier assignment length: Two months
Luggage restrictions: One carry-on and one checked bag
Frequent flyer mileage accrued: Yes
Airlines: Major
Return date flexibility: Yes
One-way tickets available: No
Cancellation phone list: No
Last-minute discounts: No
Additional non-courier travel services: Yes
Recommended advance reservations: Two months
Earliest possible reservations: Two months
Departure taxes: No
Deposit: No
Method of payment: Cash and personal check
Credit cards accepted: Yes
Comments: I found this company to be neither friendly nor helpful. I recommend using another company, if possible. If you do decide to call, you may need to be persistent in order to get the information you need.

East West Express

Destination	R/T fare	Last-minute fare	Length of stay/Departure days
Bangkok	**$750**	**No**	**Up to 45 days Tue–Sat**
Beijing	**$750**	**No**	**Up to 45 days Tue–Sat**
Hong Kong	**$750**	**No**	**Up to 45 days Tue–Sat**
Manila	**$750**	**No**	**Up to 45 days Tue–Sat**
Melbourne	**$1,250**	**$1,000**	**Up to 45 days Tue–Sat**
Singapore	**$750**	**No**	**Up to 45 days Tue–Sat**
Sydney	**$1,250**	**$1,000**	**Up to 45 days Tue–Sat**
Taipei	**$750**	**No**	**Up to 45 days Tue–Sat**
Tokyo	**$750**	**No**	**Up to 45 days Tue–Sat**

Flights originating from: New York
Address: P.O. Box 30849
City/State/Zip: Jamaica, NY 11430
Phone: 718-656-6242
Toll-free number: No
Point of contact: Tracy Arato
Times to call: 9AM–5PM EST Mon–Fri
Recorded information: No
Type of business: Courier company
Conducting business since: 1987
Annual registration fee: No
Courier assignment length: Flexible
Luggage restrictions: Carry-on only
Frequent flyer mileage accrued: Yes
Airlines used: Northwest, South African Airways
Return date flexibility: Yes—very flexible
One-way tickets available: No
Cancellation phone list: No
Last-minute discounts: No
Additional non-courier travel services: No
Recommended advance reservations: Two months
Earliest possible reservations: Three months
Departure taxes: Included
Deposit: No
Method of payment: Certified check, money order, cash, personal check
Credit cards accepted: No
Comments: This is a helpful company. Their fares do not change much throughout the year.

Halbart Express

Destination	R/T fare	Last-minute fare	Length of stay/Departure days
Brussels	**$350**	**$99**	**1 week Mon–Thu, Sat**
Copenhagen	**$150**	**$99**	**1 week Mon–Thu, Sat**
Frankfurt	**$200**	**$99**	**8 days Mon–Thu, Sat**
London	**$200**	**$99**	**1 week Mon–Thu, Sat**
Madrid	**$200**	**$99**	**1 week Mon–Thu, Sat**
Manila	**$528–$650**	**$187**	**2 weeks**
Milan	**$200**	**$149**	**2 weeks Mon–Thu, Sat**
Paris	**$200**	**$99**	**1 week Mon–Thu**
Rome	**$250**	**$99**	**8 or 9 days Tue–Thu, Sat**
Seoul	**$528–$650**	**$187**	**2 weeks**
Singapore	**$528–$650**	**$187**	**2 weeks**
Stockholm	**$200**	**$99**	**1 week Mon–Thu, Sat**
Tokyo	**$528–$650**	**$187**	**2 weeks**
Zurich	**$350**	**$150**	**1 week Mon–Thu, Sat**

Flights originating from: New York
Address: 147-05 176th Street
City/State/Zip: Jamaica, NY 11434
Phone: 718-656-8189
Fax: 718-244-0559
Toll-free number: No
Point of contact: Jeannie, Stephanie, or Amanda
Times to call: 9AM–3PM EST Mon–Fri
Recorded information: Yes, 24 hours
Type of business: Courier company
Conducting business since: 1983
Annual registration fee: No
Courier assignment length: One–two weeks
Luggage restrictions: Carry-on only
Frequent flyer mileage accrued: Yes
Airlines used: American, TWA, Asiana, Northwest
Return date flexibility: No
One-way tickets available: Yes, sometimes
Cancellation phone list: Yes
Last-minute discounts: Yes
Additional non-courier travel services: No
Recommended advance reservations: Two months
Earliest possible reservations: Two months
Departure taxes: $28
Deposit: $100
Method of payment: Certified check, money order, cash
Credit cards accepted: No
Comments: Prices are slightly higher during summer months. Halbart is one of the major players in the courier business.

Jupiter Air

Destination	R/T fare	Last-minute fare	Length of stay/Departure days
Hong Kong	**$753**	**$200**	**15–30 days Tue–Sat**
London	**$150**	**$99**	**Tue–Sat**
Singapore	**$753**	**$200**	**15–30 days Tue–Sat**

Flights originating from: New York
Address: JFK International Airport, Building 14
City/State/Zip: Jamaica, NY 11430
Phone: 718-656-6050
Fax: 718-656-7263
Toll-free number: No
Point of contact: Marilyn Cancel
Times to call: 9AM–5:30PM EST Mon–Fri
Recorded information: No
Type of business: Courier company
Conducting business since: 1988
Annual registration fee: $35
Courier assignment length: One–two weeks
Luggage restrictions: Carry-on only to Singapore; one bag to Hong Kong
Frequent flyer mileage accrued: No
Airlines used: JAL
Return date flexibility: No
One-way tickets available: No
Cancellation phone list: Yes
Last-minute discounts: Yes
Additional non-courier travel services: No
Recommended advance reservations: Two months
Earliest possible reservations: Two months
Departure taxes: No
Deposit: $100
Method of payment: Certified check, money order, cash, personal check
Credit cards accepted: No
Comments: Prices are slightly higher during summer months. This is a helpful company. As Marilyn stated, "If we do not have a person within two days prior to the flight, we will give the ticket away for FREE." It's hard to do better than that!

Now Voyager

Destination	R/T fare	Last-minute fare	Length of stay/Departure days
Bangkok	$559–$799	$299	2 weeks Tue–Thu, Sat
Buenos Aires	$499	$150	8–13 days Mon, Wed, Thu, Sat
Caracas	$240	$99	6–7 days Sat
Copenhagen	$199	$99	1 week Mon–Thu, Sat
Dublin	$359	$200	7–8 days
Frankfurt	$259	$150	7 days
Hong Kong	$559–$799	$199	3–30 days Tue–Sat
Johannesburg	$1,079	$499	Up to 45 days Wed, Fri, Sat
London	$299	$150	1 week 6 flights per day
Madrid	$299	$150	7–15 days
Manila	$559–$799	$299	3–30 days
Mexico City	$249	$100	4, 5, or 8 days Mon–Sun
Milan	$259	$149	1–2 weeks
Paris	$259	$99	1 week
Rio de Janeiro	$580	$299	1–2 weeks
Rome	$299	$99	1–2 weeks
San Juan, PR	$259	$150	6–9 days
Sao Paulo	$510	$200	Varies
Singapore	$559–$799	$150	2 weeks Mon–Sat
Stockholm	$259	$150	3–30 days
Tokyo	$559–$799	$299	3–30 days

Flights originating from: New York
Address: 74 Varick Street, Suite 307
City/State/Zip: New York, NY 10013
Phone: 212-431-1616
Fax: 212-334-5243 or 212-219-1753
Toll-free number: No
Point of contact: Anyone
Times to call: 10AM–5:30PM Mon–Fri, 12PM–4:30PM Sat EST
Recorded information: 11:00AM–5:30PM EST Mon–Fri
Type of business: Courier broker
Conducting business since: 1983
Annual registration fee: $50
Courier assignment length: One week–two months; some flights have open return dates
Luggage restrictions: Carry-on only
Frequent flyer mileage accrued: Yes
Airlines used: American, Iberia, JAL, SAS
Return date flexibility: Yes
One-way tickets available: Yes
Cancellation phone list: Yes (Jet-setter program)

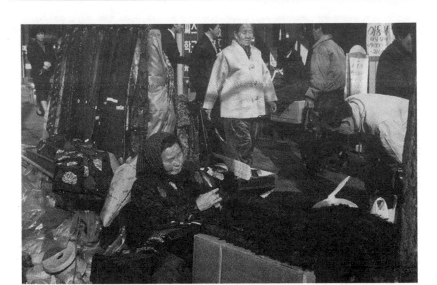

Last-minute discounts: Yes—one of the best selections in the industry
Additional non-courier travel services: Non-courier discount domestic flights
Recommended advance reservations: Two months
Earliest possible reservations: Three months
Departure taxes: No
Deposit: $100 for most flights
Method of payment: Cash, money order, cashier's check
Credit cards accepted: Yes
Comments: This is an extremely busy company and it is usually difficult to get through on the phone. They offer one of the largest selections of courier flights in the world. Be sure to call the information line prior to talking with an agent. Prices are slightly higher during summer months.

Rush Courier

Destination	R/T fare	Last-minute fare	Length of stay/Departure days
San Juan, PR	**$225**	**Free**	**3–30 days Mon–Fri**

Flights originating from: New York
Address: JFK International Airport, Building 14
City/State/Zip: Brooklyn, NY 11220
Phone: 718-656-6050
Fax: 718-656-6050
Toll-free number: 800-521-0252
Point of contact: Eileen Martinez
Times to call: 9AM–5PM EST Mon–Fri
Recorded information: No
Type of business: Courier company
Conducting business since: 1987
Annual registration fee: No
Courier assignment length: Three–thirty days
Luggage restrictions: Carry-on and one checked bag
Frequent flyer mileage accrued: Possibly—be sure to ask the airline for your mileage
Airlines used: American Airlines
Return date flexibility: Yes
One-way tickets available: Yes ($150 one way)
Cancellation phone list: Yes
Last-minute discounts: Yes
Additional non-courier travel services: No
Recommended advance reservations: One month
Earliest possible reservations: Six months
Departure taxes: No
Deposit: No
Method of payment: Certified checks, money order, cash
Credit cards accepted: No
Comments: Prices are slightly higher during summer months. This company offers good opportunities for flights to San Juan. Keep in mind that it is inexpensive to fly to other islands in the Caribbean from San Juan. Occasionally, flights will be FREE when there has been a cancellation.

World Courier

Destination	R/T fare	Last-minute fare	Length of stay/Departure days
Brussels	**$100**	**$50**	**Up to 30 days Mon–Sat**
Mexico City	**$100–$300**	**Varies**	**3–30 days Mon–Thu, Sat**
Milan	**$100–$300**	**Varies**	**9 days Mon–Fri**

Flights originating from: New York
Address: 137-42 Guy R. Brewer Boulevard
City/State/Zip: Jamaica, NY 11434
Phone: 516-354-2600
Fax: No
Toll-free number: No
Point of contact: Barbara
Times to call: 9AM–5PM EST Mon–Fri
Recorded information: No
Type of business: Courier company
Conducting business since: 1976
Annual registration fee: No
Courier assignment length: One–two weeks
Luggage restrictions: Carry-on only
Frequent flyer mileage accrued: No
Airlines used: Aeromexico, Lufthansa, Swissair
Return date flexibility: No
One-way tickets available: No
Cancellation phone list: No
Last-minute discounts: Yes
Additional non-courier travel services: No
Recommended advance reservations: One month
Earliest possible reservations: Three months
Departure taxes: Yes
Deposit: Yes
Method of payment: Certified check, money order, cash, personal check
Credit cards accepted: No
Comments: Prices are slightly higher during summer months.

SAN FRANCISCO

Virgin Express

Destination	R/T fare	Last-minute fare	Length of stay/Departure days
London	**$400**	**No**	**Up to 6 weeks daily**

Flights originating from: San Francisco
Address: Building 197, JFK International Airport
City/State/Zip: Jamaica, NY 11430
Phone: 718-244-7244
Fax: 718-244-7240
Toll-free number: No
Point of contact: Anyone
Times to call: 9AM–5PM EST Mon–Fri
Recorded information: No
Type of business: Courier broker
Conducting business since: 1991
Annual registration fee: No
Courier assignment length: Up to six weeks
Luggage restrictions: Carry-on and two pieces of luggage
Frequent flyer mileage accrued: Yes
Airlines used: Virgin
Return date flexibility: Yes
One-way tickets available: Yes
Cancellation phone list: No
Last-minute discounts: No
Additional non-courier travel services: No
Recommended advance reservations: Two months
Earliest possible reservations: Two months
Departure taxes: No
Deposit: No
Method of payment: Cash or personal check
Credit cards accepted: Yes

International Business Couriers

Destination	R/T fare	Last-minute fare	Length of stay/Departure days
Bangkok	**$495**	**Varies**	**10–14 days Tue–Sat**

Flights originating from: San Francisco
Address: 1595 E El Segundo Boulevard
City/State/Zip: El Segundo, CA 90245
Phone: 310-607-0125
Toll-free number: No
Point of contact: Anyone
Times to call: 9AM–5PM PST Mon–Fri
Recorded information: No
Type of business: Courier broker
Conducting business since: 1988
Annual registration fee: No
Courier assignment length: 10–14 days
Luggage restrictions: Carry-on only
Frequent flyer mileage accrued: Yes
Airlines used: Northwest
Return date flexibility: No
One-way tickets available: No
Cancellation phone list: No
Last-minute discounts: Yes
Additional non-courier travel services: No
Recommended advance reservations: Two months
Earliest possible reservations: Two months
Departure taxes: No
Deposit: $500
Method of payment: Cashier's check, cash, money order
Credit cards accepted: Yes

Jupiter Air

Destination	R/T fare	Last-minute fare	Length of stay/Departure days
Bangkok	$420	Varies	Varies
London	$270	Varies	Varies
Manila	$370–$420	$199	7–30 days Thu, Fri
Singapore	$385	$199	Up to 30 days Thu

Flights originating from: San Francisco
Address: 90 S Spruce Avenue
City/State/Zip: South San Francisco, CA 94080
Phone: 415-872-0845
Fax: 415-871-4975
Toll-free number: No
Point of contact: Haley Liu
Times to call: 9AM–5PM PST Mon–Fri
Recorded information: No
Type of business: Courier company
Conducting business since: 1988
Annual registration fee: $35
Courier assignment length: One–two weeks
Luggage restrictions: Carry-on only to Singapore; one bag to Hong Kong and Seoul
Frequent flyer mileage accrued: No
Airlines used: JAL, Singapore, Asiana
Return date flexibility: No
One-way tickets available: No
Cancellation phone list: Yes
Last-minute discounts: Yes
Additional non-courier travel services: No
Recommended advance reservations: Two months
Earliest possible reservations: Three months
Departure taxes: No
Deposit: $100
Method of payment: Certified check, money order, cash, personal check
Credit cards accepted: No
Comments: Prices are slightly higher during summer months.

UTL Travel

Destination	R/T fare	Last-minute fare	Length of stay/Departure days
Hong Kong	**$400**	**$100**	**Up to 30 days Tue–Sat**
Manila	**$485**	**$100**	**7–30 days Thu, Fri**
Singapore	**$335**	**$100**	**Up to 30 days Thu only**

Flights originating from: San Francisco
Address: 320 Corey Way
City/State/Zip: South San Francisco, CA 94080
Phone: 415-583-5074
Fax: 415-583-8122
Toll-free number: No
Point of contact: Any agent
Times to call: 9AM–6PM PST Mon–Fri
Recorded information: Yes
Type of business: Courier broker
Conducting business since: 1988
Annual registration fee: No
Courier assignment length: One–two weeks
Luggage restrictions: Carry-on only to Singapore; one bag to Hong Kong and Manila
Frequent flyer mileage accrued: No
Airlines used: JAL, Singapore, Asiana
Return date flexibility: No
One-way tickets available: No
Cancellation phone list: Yes
Last-minute discounts: Yes
Additional non-courier travel services: No
Recommended advance reservations: Two months
Earliest possible reservations: Three months
Departure taxes: No
Deposit: $100 or $200
Method of payment: Certified check, money order, cash, personal check
Credit cards accepted: No
Comments: Prices are slightly higher during summer months.

PUERTO RICO

SAN JUAN

Rush Courier

Destination	R/T fare	Last-minute fare	Length of stay/Departure days
New York	**$225**	**Varies**	**3-30 days Tue-Sat**

Flights originating from: San Juan
Address: 481 49th Street
City/State/Zip: Brooklyn, NY 11220
Phone: 718-439-8181
Fax: 718-656-6050
Toll-free number: 800-521-0252
Point of contact: Eileen Martinez
Times to call: 9AM–5PM EST Mon–Fri
Recorded information: No
Type of business: Courier company
Conducting business since: 1987
Annual registration fee: No
Courier assignment length: Three–thirty days
Luggage restrictions: Carry-on only
Frequent flyer mileage accrued: Yes
Airlines used: American Airlines
Return date flexibility: Yes
One-way tickets available: No
Cancellation phone list: Yes
Last-minute discounts: Yes
Additional non-courier travel services: No
Recommended advance reservations: One month
Earliest possible reservations: Six months
Departure taxes: No
Deposit: No

CANADA

MONTREAL

F. B. On Board Courier Services, Inc.

Destination	R/T fare	Last-minute fare	Length of stay/Departure days
London	$450	Varies	8, 10, 12, 14 days Mon–Thu, Sat

Flights originating from: Montreal
Address: 10225 Ryan Avenue
City/State/Zip: Dorval, Quebec H9P 1A2
Phone: 514-631-7925
Fax: No
Toll-free number: No
Point of contact: Monica or Sam Zahabi
Times to call: 9AM–12PM EST Mon–Fri
Recorded information: No
Type of business: Courier company
Conducting business since: 1988
Annual registration fee: No
Courier assignment length: Eight–fourteen days
Luggage restrictions: Carry-on only
Frequent flyer mileage accrued: Yes
Airlines used: Air Canada
Return date flexibility: No
One-way tickets available: No
Cancellation phone list: No
Last-minute discounts: Yes
Additional non-courier travel services: Yes
Recommended advance reservations: Four–six weeks
Earliest possible reservations: Three months
Departure taxes: No
Deposit: No
Method of payment: Cash, money order, cashier's check
Credit cards accepted: Only accepted 24–48 hours before flight
Comments: Prices are slightly higher during summer months. Prices are in Canadian dollars.

Jet Services

Destination	R/T fare	Last-minute fare	Length of stay/Departure days
Paris	**$395**	**$350**	**1–2 weeks Mon–Th, Sat**

Flights originating from: Montreal
Address: 2735 Paulus Street
City/State/Zip: Ville St. Laurent
Phone: 514-331-7470
Fax: 514-331-3451
Toll-free number: 800-361-4969 (Canada only)
Point of contact: Carlos Cifuentes
Times to call: 9AM–12PM and 1PM–3PM EST Mon–Fri
Recorded information: No
Type of business: Courier company
Conducting business since: 1986
Annual registration fee: No
Courier assignment length: One–two weeks
Luggage restrictions: Carry-on only
Frequent flyer mileage accrued: Yes
Airlines used: Air Canada, Air France
Return date flexibility: No
One-way tickets available: No
Cancellation phone list: No
Last-minute discounts: No
Additional non-courier travel services: No
Recommended advance reservations: One month
Earliest possible reservations: Six months
Departure taxes: No
Deposit: No
Method of payment: Cash, money order
Credit cards accepted: No
Comments: Prices are slightly higher during summer months. Prices are in Canadian dollars.

TORONTO

F. B. On Board Courier Services, Inc.

Destination	R/T fare	Last-minute fare	Length of stay/Departure days
London	**$525**	**$450**	**8, 10, 12, 14 days Mon–Thu, Sat**

Flights originating from: Toronto
Address: 10225 Ryan Avenue
City/State/Zip: Dorval, Quebec H9P 1A2
Phone: 514-631-7925
Fax: No
Toll-free number: No
Point of contact: Mary Jo
Times to call: 9AM–12PM EST Mon–Fri
Recorded information: No
Type of business: Courier company
Conducting business since: 1988
Annual registration fee: No
Courier assignment length: Eight–twelve days
Luggage restrictions: Carry-on only
Frequent flyer mileage accrued: Yes
Airlines used: Air Canada
Return date flexibility: No
One-way tickets available: No
Cancellation phone list: No
Last-minute discounts: Yes
Additional non-courier travel services: Yes
Recommended advance reservations: Four–six weeks
Earliest possible reservations: Three months
Departure taxes: No
Deposit: No
Method of payment: Cash, money order, cashier's check
Credit cards accepted: Only 24–48 hours before flight
Comments: Prices are slightly higher during summer months. Prices are in Canadian dollars.

VANCOUVER

F. B. On Board Courier Services, Inc.

Destination	R/T fare	Last-minute fare	Length of stay/Departure days
Hong Kong	**$700**	**Varies**	**1–3 weeks Tue–Sat**
London	**$570**	**Varies**	**10–15 days Tue–Sat**

Flights originating from: Vancouver
Address: 5200 Miller Road, Suite 117
City/State/Zip: Richmond, BC V7B 1X8
Phone: 604-278-1266
Fax: 604-278-5367
Toll-free number: No
Point of contact: Anyone
Times to call: 9AM–11PM or 2PM–4PM PST Mon–Fri
Recorded information: No
Type of business: Courier company
Conducting business since: 1981
Annual registration fee: No
Courier assignment length: Seven–thirty days
Luggage restrictions: Carry-on only
Frequent flyer mileage accrued: Yes
Airlines used: Air Canada, Canadian
Return date flexibility: No
One-way tickets available: No
Cancellation phone list: No
Last-minute discounts: Yes
Additional non-courier travel services: Yes
Recommended advance reservations: Three months
Earliest possible reservations: Six months
Departure taxes: $15
Deposit: No
Method of payment: Cash, money order, cashier's check
Credit cards accepted: No
Comments: Prices are slightly higher during summer months. Prices are in Canadian dollars. Book these flights early.

MEXICO

MEXICO CITY

Film Freight International

Destination	R/T fare	Last-minute fare	Length of stay/Departure days
Mexico City	**$250**	**Varies**	**Up to 1 month**

Flights originating from: Miami
Address: 8900 Bellance Avenue
City/State/Zip: Los Angeles, CA 90045
Phone: 310-568-8403
Toll-free number: No
Point of contact: Milton
Times to call: 9AM–5PM PST
Recorded information: No
Type of business: Courier broker
Conducting business since: 1984
Annual registration fee: No
Courier assignment length: Up to one month
Luggage restrictions: Carry-on only
Frequent flyer mileage accrued: Yes
Airlines used: Lacsa
Return date flexibility: Yes
One-way tickets available: No
Cancellation phone list: Yes
Last-minute discounts: Yes
Additional non-courier travel services: No
Recommended advance reservations: One month
Earliest possible reservations: One month
Departure taxes: No
Deposit: $100 non-refundable
Method of payment: Cash or personal check
Credit cards accepted: No
Comments: These flights are irregular. Please call to find out when flights depart.

GUATEMALA

GUATEMALA CITY

Trans Air Systems

Destination	R/T fare	Last-minute fare	Length of stay/Departure days
Miami	**$280**	**$180**	**30 days Tue-Sat**

Flights originating from: Guatemala City
Address: 7264 NW 25th Street
City/State/Zip: Miami, FL 33122
Phone: 305-592-1771
Fax: 305-592-2927
Toll-free number: No
Point of contact: Gloria
Times to call: 9:30AM –5:30PM EST Mon–Fri
Recorded information: No
Type of business: Courier company
Conducting business since: 1988
Annual registration fee: No
Courier assignment length: 30 days
Luggage restrictions: Carry-on only
Frequent flyer mileage accrued: Yes
Airlines used: American
Return date flexibility: No
One-way tickets available: Yes, for US citizens only
Cancellation phone list: No
Last-minute discounts: Yes
Additional non-courier travel services: No
Recommended advance reservations: One month; two months in the summer
Earliest possible reservations: Three months
Departure taxes: No
Deposit: $50
Method of payment: Money order, cash
Credit cards accepted: No
Comments: Prices are higher in the summer months. They speak Spanish.

SOUTH AMERICA

COURIER COMPANY LISTINGS

ARGENTINA

BUENOS AIRES

Trans Air Systems

Destination	R/T fare	Last-minute fare	Length of stay/Departure days
Miami	**$500**	**Varies**	**30 days Mon–Fri**

Flights originating from: Buenos Aires
Address: 7264 NW 25th Street
City/State/Zip: Miami, FL 33122
Phone: 305-592-1771
Fax: 305-592-2927
Toll-free number: No
Point of contact: Gloria
Times to call: 9:30AM –5:30PM EST Mon–Fri
Recorded information: No
Type of business: Courier company
Conducting business since: 1988
Annual registration fee: No
Courier assignment length: 30 days
Luggage restrictions: Carry-on only
Frequent flyer mileage accrued: Yes
Airlines used: Ladeco
Return date flexibility: No
One-way tickets available: Yes, for US citizens only
Cancellation phone list: No
Last-minute discounts: Yes
Additional non-courier travel services: No
Recommended advance reservations: One month; two months in the summer
Earliest possible reservations: Two months
Departure taxes: No
Deposit: $50
Method of payment: Money order, cash
Credit cards accepted: No
Comments: Prices are higher in the summer months. They speak Spanish.

MENDOZA

Trans Air Systems

Destination	R/T fare	Last-minute fare	Length of stay/Departure days
Miami	**$500**	**Varies**	**30 days Mon-Fri**

Flights originating from: Mendoza
Address: 7264 NW 25th Street
City/State/Zip: Miami, FL 33122
Phone: 305-592-1771
Fax: 305-592-2927
Toll-free number: No
Point of contact: Gloria
Times to call: 9:30AM –5:30PM EST Mon–Fri
Recorded information: No
Type of business: Courier company
Conducting business since: 1988
Annual registration fee: No
Courier assignment length: 30 days
Luggage restrictions: Carry-on only
Frequent flyer mileage accrued: Yes
Airlines used: Ladeco
Return date flexibility: No
One-way tickets available: Yes, for US citizens only
Cancellation phone list: No
Last-minute discounts: Yes
Additional non-courier travel services: No
Recommended advance reservations: One month
Earliest possible reservations: Two months
Departure taxes: No
Deposit: $50
Method of payment: Money order, cash
Credit cards accepted: No
Comments: Prices are higher in the summer months. They speak Spanish.

ECUADOR

QUITO

Trans Air Systems

Destination	R/T fare	Last-minute fare	Length of stay/Departure days
Miami	**$395**	**Varies**	**21 days Tue-Sat**

Flights originating from: Quito
Address: 7264 NW 25th Street
City/State/Zip: Miami, FL 33122
Phone: 305-592-1771
Fax: 305-592-2927
Toll-free number: No
Point of contact: Gloria
Times to call: 9:30AM–5:30PM EST Mon–Fri
Recorded information: No
Type of business: Courier company
Conducting business since: 1988
Annual registration fee: No
Courier assignment length: 21 days
Luggage restrictions: Carry-on only
Frequent flyer mileage accrued: Yes
Airlines used: American
Return date flexibility: No
One-way tickets available: Yes, for US citizens only
Cancellation phone list: No
Last-minute discounts: Yes
Additional non-courier travel services: No
Recommended advance reservations: One month; two months for summer
Earliest possible reservations: Three months
Departure taxes: No
Deposit: $50
Method of payment: Money order, cash
Credit cards accepted: No
Comments: Prices are higher in the summer months. They speak Spanish.

PACIFIC RIM

COURIER COMPANY LISTINGS

AUSTRALIA

SYDNEY

Jupiter Air

Destination	R/T fare	Last-minute fare	Length of stay/Departure days
London	$1,500–$1,600	Varies	Up to 2 months 3 flights per day

Flights originating from: Sydney
Phone: 011-61-2-317-2230
Point of contact: Bonnie
Type of business: Courier company
Conducting business since: 1988
Annual registration fee: No
Courier assignment length: Up to two months
Luggage restrictions: Carry-on only
One-way tickets available: Yes
Recommended advance reservations: Three months
Earliest possible reservations: Three months
Departure taxes: No
Deposit: $100
Method of payment: Cash, cashier's check, money order
Credit cards accepted: No
Comments: Fares are listed in Australian dollars.

HONG KONG

Airtropolis Express

Destination	R/T fare	Last-minute fare	Length of stay/Departure days
Singapore	$2,200	No	Up to 30 days
Kuala Lumpur	$2,600	No	Up to 30 days
Jakarta	$2,800	No	Up to 3 months
London	$5,200	No	Up to 1 year

Flights originating from: Hong Kong
Address: 315 Air Cargo Terminal Office Building
City/State/Zip: Hong Kong International Airport, Hong Kong
Phone: 011-852-2751-6186
Fax: 011-852-2755-8467
Toll-free number: No
Point of contact: Elaine
Times to call: 9AM to 5:30PM Hong Kong time
Recorded information: No
Type of business: Courier company
Annual registration fee: No
Courier assignment length: One month–one year
Luggage restrictions: Carry-on only for outbound; check one bag on return flight
Frequent flyer mileage accrued: No
Airlines used: Singapore Air
Return date flexibility: Yes
One-way tickets available: Only to Singapore
Cancellation phone list: No
Last-minute discounts: No
Additional non-courier travel services: No
Recommended advance reservations: One month
Earliest possible reservations: One month
Departure taxes: No
Deposit: $1,000
Method of payment: Check or cash
Credit cards accepted: No
Comments: Fares are listed in Honk Kong dollars.

Bridges Worldwide

Destination	R/T fare	Last-minute fare	Length of stay/Departure days
Bangkok	$1,000	$500	Up to 21 days Tue–Sun
London	$6,000	$3,000	Up to 1 month (full luggage)
San Francisco	$4,500	$1,900	2 weeks Mon–Thu, Sat
Sydney	$6,800	$3,500	Up to 1 month (full luggage)

Flights originating from: Hong Kong
Phone: 011-852-2305-1412
Times to call: 9:30AM–5PM Hong Kong time
Point of contact: Jeanne
Type of business: Courier company
Annual registration fee: No
Courier assignment length: Up to one month
Airlines used: Singapore, Qantas, Virgin, Thai
Luggage restrictions: Carry-on only, except for London and Sydney
Return date flexibility: No
One-way tickets available: Yes
Cancellation phone list: Yes
Last-minute discounts: Yes
Additional non-courier travel services: No
Recommended advance reservations: Three months
Earliest possible reservations: Six months
Departure taxes: No
Deposit: No
Method of payment: Cash, cashier's check, money order
Credit cards accepted: No
Comments: Fares are listed in Hong Kong dollars.

Jupiter Air

Destination	R/I fare	Last-minute fare	Length of stay/Departure days
Bangkok	**$800**	**$500**	**Up to 14 days Tue–Sun**
London	**$5,000**	**$3,500**	**Up to 1 month**
Los Angeles	**$3,800**	**$1,500**	**Up to 1 month**
New York	**$5,500**	**$2,500**	**Up to 1 month**
Singapore	**$2,100**	**$1,000**	**Up to 1 month**
Vancouver	**$5,000**	**$2,000**	**Up to 1 month**

Flights originating from: Hong Kong
Phone: 011-65-545-2921
Type of business: Courier company
Conducting business since: 1988
Annual registration fee: No
Courier assignment length: Up to one month
Luggage restrictions: Some flights allow luggage to be checked
Return date flexibility: No
One-way tickets available: No
Cancellation phone list: Yes
Last-minute discounts: Yes
Additional non-courier travel services: No
Recommended advance reservations: Three months
Earliest possible reservations: Six months
Departure taxes: No
Deposit: $1,000–$2,500 deposit (Hong Kong dollars)
Method of payment: Cash, cashier's check, money order
Credit cards accepted: No
Comments: Fares are listed in Hong Kong dollars.

Linehaul Express

Destination	R/T fare	Last-minute fare	Length of stay/Departure days
Bangkok	$1,500	$500	1 week daily
Frankfurt	$6,200	$3,500	1–30 days daily
London	$5,500	$3,000	7–30 days daily
Manchester	$6,000– $7,000	Varies	7–30 days
Manila	$900	$500	1 week daily
Osaka	$2,000	$1,000	5–14 days
Seoul	$1,500	$500	4–10 days
Singapore	$2,000	$1,000	4–30 days
Sydney	$5,800	$3,500	Up to 1 month
Taipei	$1,200	$500	Up to 1 month daily
Tokyo	$2,500	$900	Up to 1 month

Flights originating from: Hong Kong
Address: 33 Canton Road
City: Hong Kong
Phone: 011-852-2317-7347
Fax: 011-852-2735-2167
Times to call: 9:30AM-5:30PM Hong Kong time
Point of contact: Matthew Chan
Type of business: Courier company
Conducting business since: 1989
Annual registration fee: No
Courier assignment length: Up to one month
Airlines used: Cathay Pacific
Luggage restrictions: Carry-on only
Return date flexibility: Yes
One-way tickets available: No
Cancellation phone list: Yes
Last-minute discounts: Yes
Additional non-courier travel services: No
Recommended advance reservations: Three months
Earliest possible reservations: Six months
Departure taxes: No
Deposit: $2,000 deposit (Hong Kong dollars)
Method of payment: Cash, cashier's check, money order
Credit cards accepted: No
Comments: Fares are listed in Hong Kong dollars.

JAPAN

TOKYO

Fastlink Express

Destination	R/T fare	Last-minute fare	Length of stay/Departure days
Singapore	**¥40,000**	**No**	**Up to 90 days**
Hong Kong	**¥30,000**	**No**	**Up to 90 days**
Bangkok	**¥35,000**	**No**	**Up to 90 days**

Flights originating from: Tokyo
Address: 654-207, Nanaei, Tomisato-Machi, Inbu-Gun, Chiba-Pre
City/State/Zip: Tokyo 108, Japan
Phone: 011-81-4-7691-2895
Fax: 011-81-4-7691-0313
Toll-free number: No
Point of contact: Mr. A. Kukinorno
Times to call: 9AM–5PM Tokyo time
Recorded information: No
Type of business: Courier company
Annual registration fee: No
Courier assignment length: 90 days
Luggage restrictions: No
Frequent flyer mileage accrued: Yes
Airlines used: Northwest
Return date flexibility: Yes
One-way tickets available: No
Cancellation phone list: No
Last-minute discounts: No
Additional non-courier travel services: No
Recommended advance reservations: One to two months
Earliest possible reservations: Two months
Departure taxes: No
Deposit: No
Method of payment: Cash only
Credit cards accepted: No

Wholesale Courier

Destination	R/T fare	Last-minute fare	Length of stay/Departure days
Bangkok	**¥35,000**	**No**	**Up to 3 months daily**
Hong Kong	**¥35,000**	**No**	**Up to 3 months daily**
Singapore	**¥35,000**	**No**	**Up to 3 months daily**

Flights originating from: Tokyo
Address: Tsumatsu Building, 2nd Floor, 2-0-10 Hiyoshidai, Tomisato Inba-Gun
City/State/Zip: Chiba 286-02
Phone: 011-81-4-7692-0311
Fax: 011-81-47692-0309
Toll-free number: No
Point of contact: Mr. Endo
Times to call: 6PM Tokyo time
Recorded information: No
Type of business: Courier company
Annual registration fee: No
Courier assignment length: Three months
Luggage restrictions: Carry-on only
Frequent flyer mileage accrued: Yes
Airlines used: Northwest
Return date flexibility: Yes
One-way tickets available: No
Cancellation phone list: Yes
Last-minute discounts: Yes; flights costing ¥10,000–¥50,000
Additional non-courier travel services: No
Earliest possible reservations: Three months
Departure taxes: ¥20,000
Deposit: No
Method of payment: Cash only
Credit cards accepted: No
Comments: This company has flights available every day.

SINGAPORE

Air United

Destination	R/T fare	Last-minute fare	Length of stay/Departure days
Los Angeles	S$900	No	Up to 30 days
San Francisco	S$900	No	Up to 30 days
London	S$1,200	No	Up to 3 months
Bangkok	S$220	No	Up to 60 days
Tokyo	S$750	No	Up to 30 days
Manila	S$500	No	Up to 30 days
Hong Kong	S$480	No	Up to 30 days

Flights originating from: Singapore
Address: 5001 Beach Road, #03-64 East Golden Mile Complex
City/State/Zip: Singapore 0719
Phone: 011-65-735-7684
Fax: 011-65-294-6094
Toll-free number: No
Point of contact: Karen Ho or Fizah
Times to call: 10AM–6PM Singapore time
Recorded information: No
Type of business: Courier company
Annual registration fee: No
Courier assignment length: One–three months
Luggage restrictions: Can check one bag
Frequent flyer mileage accrued: No, except on Qantas
Airlines used: UA, JAL, Qantas, and Singapore Air
Return date flexibility: No
One-way tickets available: Yes, for some flights
Cancellation phone list: No
Last-minute discounts: Yes
Additional non-courier travel services: No
Recommended advance reservations: One month
Earliest possible reservations: Two–three months
Departure taxes: No
Deposit: S$150–S$250
Method of payment: Cash or check
Credit cards accepted: No
Comments: Fares are listed in Singapore dollars.

Bridges Worldwide

Destination	R/T fare	Last-minute fare	Length of stay/Departure days
Bangkok	**S$200**	**No**	**Up to 14 days**

Flights originating from: Singapore
Address: SATS Air Freight Terminal, Module 1A, Second Floor, Room 203
City/State/Zip: Changi Airport, Singapore 1781
Phone: 011-65-545-4327
Fax: 011-65-543-0258
Toll-free number: No
Point of contact: Shida
Times to call: 9AM–6PM Singapore time
Recorded information: No
Type of business: Courier company
Annual registration fee: No
Courier assignment length: Two weeks
Luggage restrictions: Carry-on luggage of 20kg only
Frequent flyer mileage accrued: Yes
Airlines used: Scandinavian Airlines
Return date flexibility: Yes
One-way tickets available: $100
Cancellation phone list: No
Last-minute discounts: Yes
Additional non-courier travel services: No
Recommended advance reservations: Two–four weeks
Earliest possible reservations: Two months
Departure taxes: $15
Deposit: No
Method of payment: Cash only
Credit cards accepted: No
Comments: Fares are listed in Singapore dollars.

TNT Travel

Destination	R/T fare	Last-minute fare	Length of stay/Departure days
Los Angeles	**S$850**	**No**	**Up to 1 month**

Flights originating from: Singapore
Address: 12 Prince Edward Road, Unit 06-03 Podium B
City/State/Zip: Singapore 079212
Phone: 011-65-222-7255
Fax: 011-65-225-1654
Toll-free number: No
Point of contact: Eileen
Times to call: 8AM–6PM Singapore time
Recorded information: No
Type of business: Courier company
Annual registration fee: No
Courier assignment length: One month
Luggage restrictions: Check in one piece totaling 20kg; return check in 30kg
Frequent flyer mileage accrued: Yes
Airlines used: Northwest
Return date flexibility: Yes
One-way tickets available: No
Cancellation phone list: No
Last-minute discounts: No
Additional non-courier travel services: No
Recommended advance reservations: One month
Earliest possible reservations: One–two months
Departure taxes: No
Deposit: S$500
Method of payment: Cashier's check, cash, money order
Credit cards accepted: Yes
Comments: Fares are listed in Singapore dollars.

THAILAND

BANGKOK

OBC Courier

Destination	R/T fare	Last-minute fare	Length of stay/Departure days
Singapore	**B3,500**	**No**	**Up to 14 days**

Flights originating from: Bangkok
Address: Vanit Building #1, 16th Floor, Room 1605, 1126/1 New Petchburi Road
City/State/Zip: Bangkok 10400 Thailand
Phone: 011-66-2-255-8590
Fax: 011-66-2-225-8593
Toll-free number: No
Point of contact: Charlie
Times to call: 9AM–6PM Bangkok time
Recorded information: No
Type of business: Courier company
Annual registration fee: No
Courier assignment length: Fourteen days
Luggage restrictions: Carry-on only
Frequent flyer mileage accrued: Yes
Airlines used: Singapore Air
Return date flexibility: Yes
One-way tickets available: Yes
Cancellation phone list: No
Last-minute discounts: No
Additional non-courier travel services: No
Earliest possible reservations: One month. Must pay 10 days in advance.
Departure taxes: B20
Deposit: No
Method of payment: Cash only
Credit cards accepted: No
Comments: Must book 10 days in advance. Fares are listed in Baht.

Siam Trans International

Destination	R/T fare	Last-minute fare	Length of stay/Departure days
Singapore	**B3,500**	**No**	**Up to 14 days**
Hong Kong	**B3,500**	**No**	**Up to 14 days**

Flights originating from: Bangkok
Address: 78 Kiatnakin Building, Bushland, New Road
City/State/Zip: Bangkok 10500 Thailand
Phone: 011-66-2-235-6741
Fax: 011-66-2-236-1042
Toll-free number: No
Point of contact: Sirirat
Times to call: 10AM–6PM Bangkok time
Recorded information: No
Type of business: Courier company
Annual registration fee: No
Courier assignment length: Up to 14 days
Luggage restrictions: Carry-on only
Frequent flyer mileage accrued: No
Airlines used: Thai, Singapore
Return date flexibility: Yes
One-way tickets available: Yes
Cancellation phone list: No
Last-minute discounts: No
Additional non-courier travel services: No
Recommended advance reservations: Two weeks
Earliest possible reservations: One month
Departure taxes: No
Deposit: No
Method of payment: Cash only
Credit cards accepted: No
Comments: It's best to check availability on the first of each month. Fares are listed in Baht.

EUROPE

COURIER COMPANY LISTINGS

UNITED KINGDOM

LONDON

Bridges Worldwide

Destination	R/T fare	Last-minute fare	Length of stay/Departure days
Bangkok	£325	£99	Up to 2 months Tue–Sat
Los Angeles	£300	£99	Up to 2 months Tue–Sat
Newark	£200	£99	Up to 2 months Tue–Sat
New York	£200	£99	Up to 2 months Tue–Sat
San Francisco	£300	£99	Up to 2 months Tue–Sat
Tokyo	£325	£99	Up to 2 months Tue–Sat

Flights originating from: London
Address: Old Mill Road House
City/State/Zip: West Drayton, Middlesex TW3 3JU
Phone: 011-441-895-465-065
Toll-free number: No
Point of contact: Stuart
Times to call: 9AM–5PM GMT
Recorded information: No
Type of business: Courier broker
Conducting business since: 1991
Annual registration fee: No
Courier assignment length: Up to one month
Luggage restrictions: Carry-on and one checked bag
Frequent flyer mileage accrued: Yes
Airlines used: Virgin Gulf
Return date flexibility: No
One-way tickets available: Yes, sometimes
Cancellation phone list: No
Last-minute discounts: Yes
Additional non-courier travel services: Non-courier discount flights
Recommended advance reservations: Two–three months
Earliest possible reservations: Two–three months
Departure taxes: No
Deposit: No
Method of payment: Cash, cashier's check
Credit cards accepted: Yes
Comments: The company must receive full payment before your booking is confirmed. All prices are in £ sterling.

British Airways Travel Shops

Destination	R/T fare	Last-minute fare	Length of stay/Departure days
Bahrain	**£250**	**Varies**	**1–3 weeks**
Bangkok	**£348**	**Varies**	**1–3 weeks**
Barcelona	**£80**	**Varies**	**1–3 weeks**
Boston	**£180**	**Varies**	**1–3 weeks**
Buenos Aires	**£360**	**Varies**	**1–3 weeks**
Cairo	**£130**	**Varies**	**1–3 weeks**
Chicago	**£180**	**Varies**	**1–3 weeks**
Dubai	**£250**	**Varies**	**1–3 weeks**
Gaborone	**£350**	**Varies**	**1–3 weeks**
Harare	**£220**	**Varies**	**1–3 weeks**
Hong Kong	**£348**	**Varies**	**1–3 weeks**
Kuala Lumpur	**£348**	**Varies**	**1–3 weeks**
Larnaca	**£175**	**Varies**	**1–3 weeks**
Lisbon	**£80**	**Varies**	**1–3 weeks**
Los Angeles	**£250**	**Varies**	**1–3 weeks**
Mauritius	**£428**	**Varies**	**1–3 weeks**
Miami	**£150**	**Varies**	**1–3 weeks**
Montreal	**£180**	**Varies**	**1–3 weeks**
Nairobi	**£260**	**Varies**	**1–3 weeks**
New York	**£180**	**Varies**	**1–3 weeks**
Philadelphia	**£180**	**Varies**	**1–3 weeks**
San Francisco	**£250**	**Varies**	**1–3 weeks**
Seattle	**£250**	**Varies**	**1–3 weeks**
Singapore	**£348**	**Varies**	**1–3 weeks**
Tel Aviv	**£100**	**Varies**	**1–3 weeks**
Tokyo	**£498**	**Varies**	**1–3 weeks**
Toronto	**£180**	**Varies**	**1–3 weeks**
Washington, DC	**£180**	**Varies**	**1–3 weeks**

Flights originating from: London
Address: World Cargo Centre, 1st Floor, Export Cargo Terminal S126, Heathrow Airport
City/State/Zip: Hounslow, Middlesex TW6 2JS
Phone: 011-441-815-647-009
Fax: 011-441-815-626-177
Toll-free number: No
Point of contact: Reservations
Times to call: 9AM–5PM GMT
Recorded information: No
Type of business: Airline/Courier/Freight
Conducting business since: 1985
Annual registration fee: No
Courier assignment length: One–three weeks
Luggage restrictions: Carry-on and luggage
Frequent flyer mileage accrued: Yes

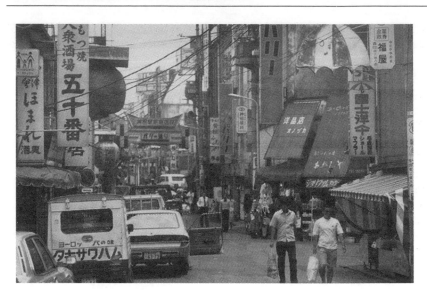

Airlines used: British Airways
Return date flexibility: No
One-way tickets available: No
Cancellation phone list: No
Last-minute discounts: Yes
Additional non-courier travel services: Yes
Recommended advance reservations: Two–three months
Earliest possible reservations: Two–three months
Departure taxes: Included in price
Deposit: No
Method of payment: Cash, cashier's check, money order
Credit cards accepted: Yes
Comments: A dress code is strictly enforced—no jeans allowed. No refunds or cancellations are accepted. All prices are in £ sterling.

Jupiter Air UK

Destination	R/T fare	Last-minute fare	Length of stay/Departure days
New York	**£185Varies**	**No**	**Up to 2 weeks Mon-Sat**

Flights originating from: London
Address: Jupiter House, Horton Road, Coinbrook
City/State/Zip: Slough SL3 OBB
Phone: 011-44-175-368-9989
Fax: 011-44-175-368-1661
Toll-free number: No
Point of contact: Claire
Times to call: 9PM to 5PM GMT
Recorded information: No
Type of business: Courier company
Annual registration fee: No
Courier assignment length: Up to two weeks
Luggage restrictions: Carry-on luggage only
Frequent flyer mileage accrued: Yes
Airlines used: United
Return date flexibility: Yes
One-way tickets available: Yes, sometimes
Cancellation phone list: No
Last-minute discounts: Yes
Additional non-courier travel services: No
Earliest possible reservations: One to two months
Departure taxes: £10
Deposit: £100
Method of payment: Cash, Mastercard, Visa
Credit cards accepted: Yes
Comments: The staff is very helpful and friendly. This is a popular flight so try to book one month in advance.

Linehaul Express

Destination	R/T fare	fare	Length of stay/Departure days
From London:			
Hong Kong	**£250–£550**	**Varies**	**Up to 45 days Tue–Sat**
Sydney	**£380–£625**	**Varies**	**Up to 45 days Tue–Sat**
From Manchester:			
Hong Kong	**£250–£550**	**Varies**	**Up to 45 days Tue–Sat**
Sydney	**£380–£625**	**Varies**	**Up to 45 days Tue–Sat**

Flights originating from: London and Manchester
Address: Building 252, Section D, Ely Road, Heathrow Airport
City/State/Zip: Hounslow, Middlesex TW6 2PR
Phone: 011-441-81-759-5969
Fax: 011-441-81-759-5973
Toll-free number: No
Point of contact: Anyone
Times to call: 9AM–5PM GMT
Recorded information: No
Type of business: Courier broker
Conducting business since: 1989
Annual registration fee: No
Courier assignment length: Up to 45 days
Luggage restrictions: Carry-on only
Frequent flyer mileage accrued: Yes
Airlines used: Cathay Pacific
Return date flexibility: No
One-way tickets available: No
Cancellation phone list: No
Last-minute discounts: No
Additional non-courier travel services: Yes
Recommended advance reservations: Two months
Earliest possible reservations: Two months
Departure taxes: No
Deposit: £100
Method of payment: Cash, cashier's check
Credit cards accepted: Yes
Comments: All prices are in £ sterling.

FRANCE

PARIS

Linehaul Express

Destination	R/T fare	Last-minute fare	Length of stay/Departure days
Hong Kong	**F4,500**	**No**	**Up to 45 days Tue–Fri**
Manila	**F4,900**	**No**	**Up to 45 days Tue–Fri**
Osaka	**F4,600**	**No**	**Up to 45 days Tue–Fri**
Seoul	**F4,900**	**No**	**Up to 45 days Tue–Fri**
Shanghai	**F4,900**	**No**	**Up to 45 days Tue–Fri**
Singapore	**F4,900**	**No**	**Up to 45 days Tue–Fri**
Sydney	**F5,300**	**No**	**Up to 45 days Tue–Fri**
Taipei	**F4,600**	**No**	**Up to 45 days Tue–Fri**
Tokyo	**F4,600**	**No**	**Up to 45 days Tue–Fri**

Flights originating from: Paris
Address: 28 Rue des Voyells, Zone de Fret 4, BP 10032, 95701
City/State/Zip: Roissy, Charles de Gaulle, Cedex
Phone: 011-331-48-64-51-38
Toll-free number: No
Point of contact: Fredric
Times to call: 9AM–5PM Paris time
Recorded information: No
Type of business: Courier broker
Conducting business since: 1990
Annual registration fee: No
Courier assignment length: Up to 45 days
Luggage restrictions: Carry-on only
Frequent flyer mileage accrued: Yes
Airlines used: Cathay Pacific
Return date flexibility: No
One-way tickets available: No
Cancellation phone list: No
Last-minute discounts: No
Additional non-courier travel services: No
Recommended advance reservations: Three weeks
Earliest possible reservations: Two months

Departure taxes: No
Deposit: £100
Method of payment: Cash, cashier's check
Credit cards accepted: Yes
Comments: The Sydney flight has a layover in Hong Kong for one evening. Linehaul pays for hotel accommodations. They are very helpful. All prices are in French francs.

GERMANY

FRANKFURT

Linehaul Express

Destination	R/T fare	Last-minute fare	Length of stay/Departure days
Bangkok	**200DM**	**No**	**Up to 3 months Tue–Sat**
Hong Kong	**800DM**	**No**	**Up to 3 months Tue–Sat**
Osaka	**450DM**	**No**	**Up to 3 months Tue–Sat**
Shanghai	**350DM**	**No**	**Up to 3 months Tue–Sat**
Singapore	**250DM**	**No**	**Up to 3 months Tue–Sat**
Taipei	**175DM**	**No**	**Up to 3 months Tue–Sat**
Tokyo	**450DM**	**No**	**Up to 3 months Tue–Sat**

Flights originating from: Frankfurt
Address: GE13, Room 5035 60549
City/State/Zip: Frankfurt, Germany
Phone: 011-49-69-6979 3260
Toll-free number: No
Point of contact: Anyone
Times to call: 9AM–5PM German time
Recorded information: No
Type of business: Courier broker
Conducting business since: 1990
Annual registration fee: No
Courier assignment length: Up to three months
Luggage restrictions: Carry-on only
Frequent flyer mileage accrued: Yes
Airlines used: Cathay Pacific
Return date flexibility: No
One-way tickets available: No
Cancellation phone list: No
Last-minute discounts: No
Additional non-courier travel services: No
Recommended advance reservations: Two months
Earliest possible reservations: Two–four months
Departure taxes: No
Deposit: No
Method of payment: Cash, cashier's check
Credit cards accepted: No
Comments: All prices are in German marks.

PART III

RESOURCES

FOR THE COURIER

The following pages provide you with a wealth of travel information. As an air courier, once you reach your destination, you'll have the same needs as other travelers. We've listed contact information for all kinds of travel-related organizations—from auto drive away companies to international hostels and hotels. We've included information on obtaining a visa and passport, as well as lists of travel companies, international tourist offices, recommended travel books, travel bookstores, and more. You can use these organizations to help you plan an exciting adventure abroad.

TRAVEL COMPANIES

The following is a list of travel companies that could save you money on international and domestic travel.

Access International, Ltd. .... (800) 917-7880

Air Brokers International, Inc. .... (800) 883-3273
Specializes in around-the-world trips.

ANZ Travel .... (800) 735-3861
Specializes in Australia and New Zealand.

Apex Travel, Inc. .... (800) 666-0025
Specializes in discount airfares to Asia.

British European Travel .... (800) 747-1476
Good fares to Europe and a very helpful company.

Express Discount Travel .... (800) 266-8669
Discounts up to 50 percent.

Using Travel Companies

Travel companies typically offer international flights for twenty to thirty percent less than normal economy fares. Although this is an economical way to travel, be aware that ticket deliveries are notoriously slow, and refunds can be made only through the travel company.

Euro-Asia Express .... (800) 782-9625
Specializes in discount airfares to Asia and Europe.

Discount Travel International .... (800) 900-7681
Up to 60 percent discounts on all types of travel.
$45 annual membership fee.

Preferred Traveler's Club .... (800) 638-8976

Europe Through the Back Door, Inc. .... (206) 771-8303
Carries many travel books.
Offers Eurail/Britrail passes, youth hostel guides, and many other services needed for European travel.

Fellowship Travel International .... (800) 446-7667
Low cost international fares.
Call between 9AM and 5PM EST.

International Students Exchange Flights .... (602) 951-1700
Specializes in low cost flights to most cities in Europe.
Offers Eurail/Britrail passes, youth hostel guides, and many other services needed for European travel.
Organization that has helped students for over 35 years.
Call for their current catalog and prices.

Japan Budget Travel .... (800) 722-0797

Last Minute Travel Club .... (800) 527-8646
Great fares from the East Coast to Europe.
Outstanding deals from the East Coast to Mexico or the Caribbean.

Maharaja Travel .... (800) 223-6862
Great fares to Europe and India.

Moment's Notice, Inc. .... (212) 486-0500

Pan Express Travel, Inc. .... (212) 719-9292

Travel Avenue .... (800) 333-3335
Heavily discounted airfares to Europe.
Around-the-world airfares for as little as $1569.

Traveler's Advantage .... (800) 548-1116
Sells unsold space on charter flights, cruises, and tours.

Uni Travel .... (800) 325-2222, (800) 325-2027, (314) 569-0900
Discounted international and domestic airfares.

Virgin Atlantic Airways .... (800) 862-8621
Usually the most inexpensive airlines to Europe.

Worldwide Discount Travel Club .... (305) 534-2082

DEPARTURE CITIES

All courier flights leave from the cities listed. It is your responsibility to get to the departure city. If you happen to live in or near New York, Los Angeles, Toronto, Miami, or San Francisco, there are ample flights departing from those cities. For the rest of us who do not live in those cities, we need to find our way to one of the many departure cities. If you live anywhere near New York (by anywhere I mean east of the Mississippi) it is to your advantage to get to New York. Your best savings are from New York. If you live in the western part of the United States, then Los Angeles or San Francisco should be your goal.

Southwest Airlines is a good option. Their fares are usually the cheapest in the United States. Call them at (800) 435-9792.

America West is another good choice for inexpensive flights. Call them at (800) 235-9292. They offer flights to New York and Los Angeles from most of the United States.

AUTO DRIVE AWAY COMPANIES

Another option is an auto drive away company. This is where you agree to transport a car for a company from one location to another. The main advantage to doing this is free transportation. You are only responsible for the gas and your expenses. It does not cost you anything to do this. The company will provide you with a free car. There are opportunities to drive expensive cars across all or part of America. If you have ever wanted to drive across the country in a Lexus, BMW, or Mercedes, this could be your chance.

Auto drive away companies give you plenty of time to get across the country. An example is eight to nine days to drive from New York to Los Angeles. This would give you an opportunity for some great sightseeing. Drivers are always in demand by drive away companies, and they can even arrange a return car after your courier flight (remember that this is why you bought this book in the first place).

This is a great opportunity to bring a couple of friends to a departure city for courier flights. Two or three people could pick up a car in one city and drop it off in New York or Los Angeles and catch a courier flight. It is possible to travel around the world for free or next to nothing. You can't do much better than that!

Auto DriveAway Company .... **(800) 346-2277**
- *85 offices nationwide; New York (212) 967-2344, Los Angeles (213) 661-6100, Chicago (312) 939-3600, Miami (305) 931-8330*
- *Drivers must be 21 years of age and have a valid driver's license.*
- *Deposits range from $250/$350 and up. It is refundable by any office and can be paid by cash or traveler's checks.*
- *Foreign drivers are welcome.*
- *Drivers are always in demand.*
- *There is a $10 nonrefundable registration fee.*

A Anthony's Driveaway and Truckaway Co., Inc.
- *Offices nationwide; New York (212) 935-8030, Los Angeles (714) 634-8848, Dallas (214) 823-2820, Denver (303) 893-6101, Washington, DC (540) 349-8471*
- *Drivers must be 25 years of age and have a valid driver's license.*
- *A deposit is required. $200 in cash required if the driver has a credit card as a reference. A deposit of $300 cash is required if the driver does not have a credit card.*
- *Passengers are allowed but must complete registration forms.*

National Auto Transporters, Inc.
- *Offices nationwide; Chicago (312) 489-3500, Miami (305) 945-4104, Los Angeles (818) 988-9000, San Diego (619) 578-3336, Phoenix (602) 992-5200*
- *Drivers must be 21 years of age and have a valid driver's license.*
- *A $250 deposit is required.*
- *Cash only.*
- *There is a $20 nonrefundable registration fee.*
- *Passengers are allowed.*

Auto Drive Away Companies: What you should know

- *You will need a valid driver's license.*
- *Most of the time you will be asked for a deposit using a credit card or cash.*
- *Some companies have age requirements.*
- *Often there will be mileage and time restrictions.*

FREIGHTER TRAVEL

Freighter travel is slow and fairly inexpensive. This type of travel is gaining in popularity once again; however, you must be flexible with your travel plans. It was this type of travel that gave us the expression "slow boat to China." The following are a couple of freighter companies:

Columbus Lines .... **(212) 432-1700**
Ships leave from both U.S. coasts destined for Australia and New Zealand.

Lykes Lines .... **(800) 535-1861**
Ships leave from the East Coast of the U.S. destined for Africa and the Mediterranean.

The following is a list of a number of the books or newsletters available on freighter travel:

Ford's Freighter Travel Guide .... **(818) 701-7414**
19488 Londelius Street, Northridge, CA 91324
$24 for an annual subscription.

Freighter Travel Club of America
3524 Harts Lake Road, Roy, WA 98580
$18 for a one-year subscription; $28 for two years.

Freighter World Cruises .... **(818) 449-3106**
9903 Oaks Lane, Seminole, FL 34642
Travel agency that specializes in freighter travel.

PASSPORTS

If you do not have a valid U.S. passport you will need to apply for one a couple of months prior to your trip. Foreigners must have a current passport from their country. A U.S. passport is valid for ten years. The current charge is $65. The fee is lower if you deal directly with one of the thirteen passport agencies listed on the next page.

It is possible to get your passport in one day; however, you must be able to show that you are leaving the country in less than seventy-two hours. This will be very difficult to do if you are traveling as a courier. For an additional charge you can have your passport in one week. Your best bet is to obtain your passport long before your date of departure. Do not wait until summer as the lines can be extremely long. If you are not located near a passport office, the main post office in your city will provide an application.

You can obtain your passport quicker by going to one of the thirteen Passport Agency Offices listed on this page.

Boston Passport Agency .... **(617) 565-6990**
10 Causeway Street, Room 247, Thomas P. O'Neil Federal Building, Boston, MA 02222

Chicago Passport Agency .... **(312) 353-7155**
Duczynski Federal Building, Room 380, 230 South Dearborn Street, Chicago, IL 60604

Honolulu Passport Agency .... **(808) 522-8283**
1312 Bishop Street, Suite 500, Honolulu, HI 96850

Houston Passport Agency .... **(713) 653-3160**
1919 Smith Street, Houston, TX 77002

Los Angeles Passport Agency .... **(310) 235-7070**
Federal Building, 11000 Wilshire Boulevard, Room 13100, Los Angeles, CA 90024-3615

Miami Passport Agency .... **(305) 536-4681**
Federal Office Building, 16th Floor, 51 SW First Avenue, Miami, FL 33130

New Orleans Passport Agency .... **(504) 589-6161**
Postal Services Building, Room T12005, 701 Loyola Avenue, New Orleans, LA 70113

New York Passport Agency .... **(212) 399-5290**
630 Fifth Avenue, New York, NY 10111-0031

Philadelphia Passport Agency .... **(215) 597-7480**
United States Custom House, 200 Chestnut Street, Room 103, Philadelphia, PA 19106

San Francisco Passport Agency .... **(415) 744-4444**
525 Market Street, San Francisco, CA 94105

Seattle Passport Agency .... **(206) 220-7788**
Federal Building, Room 992, 915 Second Avenue, Seattle, WA 98174

Stamford Passport Agency .... **(203) 325-4401**
One Landmark Square, Broad and Atlantic Streets, Stamford, CT 06901

Washington Passport Agency .... **(202) 647-0518**
111 19th Street NW, Washington, DC 20524

VISAS

A visa is an official approval for you to enter a country. Currently over half of all countries require them. You will need to consult the courier companies, airlines, consulates, or embassies about whether you will need a visa. In order to obtain one, you will have to write directly to the consulate or embassy. Some visas cost money, while others are free.

If you are interested in having someone else do the legwork for you or you are in a rush, there are a couple of companies that, for a fee, offer this service.

Express Visa Service .... **(202) 337-2442**
2150 Wisconsin Avenue, Suite 20, Washington, DC 20007

Passport Plus .... **(800) 367-1818 or (212) 759-5540**
20 E 49th Street, Third Floor, New York, NY 10017

HOSTELS AND HOTELS

Youth hostels are a wonderful way to avoid costly hotel bills and meet many interesting people. Hostels are not like hotels. Each hostel has its own individuality, but common customs pervade. They all have dormitory-style sleeping quarters and bathroom facilities separated for males and females. The rooms are furnished with bunk beds, mattresses, pillows, and blankets. Hostels have fully equipped self-service kitchens, dining rooms, and common rooms. Under the supervision of a residential manager, most hostels have a curfew at night. Hostellers may be asked to help with a small task to contribute to the hostel's upkeep, and are responsible for cleaning up after themselves. Environmental recycling practices are employed as well as a smoke-free policy. Alcohol and illegal drugs are not permitted.

Hostelling International–American Youth Hostels (HI–AYH) is a nonprofit membership organization founded in 1934 to promote international understanding by educational travel through an operating network of 6,000 hostels in 70 countries.

The mission of AYH is "To help all people, especially young people, gain a greater understanding of the world and its people." AYH is comprised of 38 local councils, each responsible for its own development, maintenance, operation, and fund-raising.

There are over 3,000 youth hostels in Europe, and over 200 in the United States. The average cost for a night is $3–$20 in Europe and $7–$30 in the United States. For more information contact an organization in the following list:

American Youth Hostel .... **(202) 737-5537**
1009 11th Street NW, Washington, DC 20001

Canadian Hostelling Association .... **(613) 237-7884**
400-205 Catherine Street, Ottawa, ON K2P 1C3

YHA England and Wales .... **(441) (71) 836-8541**
14 Southampton Street, London WC2E 7HY, England

INTERNATIONAL HOSTEL DIRECTORY

The following is a list of some inexpensive places to sleep either in the departure cities for your courier flights or just when visiting these great cities.

AMSTERDAM

Access International, Ltd. .... **(800) 825-3633**

Frisco Inn .... **(31) (20) 620-1610**
Beurst. 5, Amsterdam
f35 per person per night

Hotel Casa Cara .... **(31) (20) 662-3135**
Emmast. 24, Amsterdam
f55–95/f75–105 double per night

't Ancker .... **(31) (20) 662-9560**
De Ruijterkade 100, Amsterdam
Located near central station
f40 for dorm room per night

ATHENS

Acropolis House .... **(30) (1) 322-2344**
Voulis Kodrou 6 Street, Athens
Very elegant hotel
12,370GDR single (including breakfast)/17,850GDR double (including breakfast)

WHAT IS A HOSTEL, ANYWAY?

◆ Hostels offer a unique opportunity to make new friends and learn more about the world.

◆ Hostels offer unbeatable savings on overnight lodging. Enjoy a dormitory-style bedroom and shared bathroom for around $8–$16 per night, plus global discounts on car rentals, sports equipment, museum admissions, meals, and more!

◆ Hostels provide separate sleeping quarters for males and females. Some provide private family rooms. Beds come with blankets and pillows, while hostellers provide (or rent) their own towels and linens.

◆ Most hostels provide fully equipped, self-service kitchens. Some have laundry facilities, libraries, hot tubs, private rooms for couples and families, concierge services, and other amenities.

◆ The most extensive network of hostels is organized by the International Youth Hostel Federation. An AYH membership card provides access to all 6,000 IYHF hostels in 70 countries around the world.

◆ Hostelling International is the new seal of approval of the International Youth Hostel Federation.

◆ Hostels are set in strikingly beautiful castles, in ultramodern facilities near urban centers, or in tranquil rural settings.

◆ Hostels are open to travelers of all ages, except in the Bavarian region of Germany, where the age limit is 26.

◆ The Guide to Budget Accommodations provides up-to-date listings on all hostels. Volume 1 covers Europe and the Mediterranean region. Volume 2 covers the rest of the world. Both books are available from AYH council offices across the nation.

◆ AYH membership is valid for twelve months from the date of issue and includes a free copy of Hosteling in North America: A Guide to Hostels in Canada and the U.S.A.

Athens International Youth Hostel............................ (30) (1) 523-4170
16 Victor Hugo Street, Athens
1,500GDR per night
Members only

Pella Inn .... (30) (1) 325-0598
104 Ermou Street, Athens
Popular hotel with balcony rooms that have a great view of the Acropolis
4,000GDR single/6,000GDR double/7,000GDR triple

BANGKOK

Bangkok International Youth Hostel .... (66) (2) 281-0361
25/2 Phitsanulok Road, Sisao Theves, Dusit, Bangkok 10300
250 Baht per night

BARCELONA

Marc de deu de Montserrat .... (34) (3) 210-5151
Passeig Marc de Deu del Coll 41-51, CP 08023 Barcelona
2,075Ptas per night for members
2,375Ptas per night for non-members

Hostal de Joves.. (34) (3) 300-3104
Passeig Pujades 29, CP 08018 Barcelona
1,300Ptas per night per person under the age of 25
1,380Ptas per night per person over the age of 25
Breakfast is included

Pere Tarres .... (34) (3) 410-2309
Numancia 149, CP 08029 Barcelona
1,350Ptas per night per person
Breakfast is included

Studio .... (34) (3) 205-0961
Duquesa d'Orleans 58, CP 08034 Barcelona
This hostel is open only for the summer (June–August)

BOSTON

Boston International Youth Hostel .... (617) 536-9455
  General info line .... (617) 731-5430
12 Hemingway, Boston, MA 02115
$17 per night for members
$20 per night for non-members

BRUSSELS

Jean Nihon .... (32) (2) 410-3858
4 rue de l'Elephant, 1080 Bruxelles
  395BF per night for a dormitory room with eight people
  450BF per night for a room with four people
  550BF per night for a double
  650BF per night for a single
  Breakfast is included

Jacques Brel .... (32) (2) 218-0187
Rue de la Sablonniere 30, 1000 Bruxelles
  395BF per night for a dormitory room
  450BF per night for a room with four people
  550BF per night for a single

Bruegel .... (32) (2) 511-0436
1000 Brussel, Heilig Geestraat 2
  395 BF per night for a dormitory room
  450–550BF per night for a room with four people
  660BF per night for a single

BUENOS AIRES

Buenos Aires International Youth Hostel .... (54) (1) 362-9133
Calle Brasil 675, Buenos Aires

CHICAGO

Chicago Summer Hostel .... (312) 327-5350
731 S Plymouth Court, Chicago, IL 60605
  $19 per night for members/$34.50 per night for non-members
  (closed September 3–June 7)

International House of Chicago .... (312) 753-2270
1414 E 59th Street, Chicago, IL 60637
  $19 per night for members/$34.50 per night for non-members
  Single room accommodations

COPENHAGEN

Amager .... (45) 325 22 908
Vejlandsalle 200, 2300 Copenhagen S

Bellahoj .... **(45) 312 89 715**
Danhostel Bellahoj, Herbervejen 8, 2700 Bronshoj
70kr per night for members
95 kr per night for non-members

DUBAI

Dubai Hostel .... **(971) (4) 625 578**
Al Qusais Road, Dubai

DUBLIN

Dublin International .... **(353) (1) 830-1766**
61 Mountjoy Street, Dublin 7
7L per night for members
7L per night for non-members

Harcourt Street .... **(353) (1) 475-0430**
Harcourt Street, Dublin 2
9L per night

FRANKFURT

Haus der Jegend .... **(49) (69) 619 058**
Deuscherrnufer 12, 60594 Frankfurt
DM28 per night in a dormitory room
Members only

GUAYAQUIL

Guayaquil Youth Hostel .... **(593) (4) 248 357**
Ecuahogar, Av Isidro Ayora (Sauces I), Frente al Banco Ecuatoriano de
la Vivienda MZF31V20, Guayaquil

HONG KONG

Bradbury Hall .... **(852) 232 82 458**
Check Keng, Sai Kung Peninsula, New Territories

Ma Wui Hall .... **(852) 281 75 715**
Top of Mt. Davis Path, off Victoria Road, Kennedy Town, Hong Kong
Island
HK$50 for members
HK$75 for non-members

Jockey Club Mong Tung Wan Youth Hostel .... (852) 298 41 389
Lantau Island
HK$25 for members
HK$50 for non-members

S. G. Davis Youth Hostel .... (852) 298 55 610
Ngong Ping, Lantau Island
HK$25 for members
HK$50 for non-members

Hoi Ha Youth Hostel .... (852) 232 82 327
Hoi Ha Road, Pak Sah O, Sai Kung Peninsula
HK$25 per night

Bradbury Lodge .... (852) 266 25 123
Off Ting Kok Road, Tai Mei Tuk, Tai Po, New Territories
HK$35 per night

Sze Lok Yuen Hostel .... (852) 248 88 188
Off Tai Mo Shan Road, Tsuen Wan, New Territories

JOHANNESBURG

Fairview Hostel .... (27) (11) 618-2048
4 College Street, Fairview 2094, Johannesburg
R28 per night

Johannesburg Central Hostel .... (27) (11) 643-1213
4 Fife Avenue, Berea, Johannesburg
R25 per night for members
R28 per night for non-members

Kew Hostel .... (27) (11) 887-9072
5 Johannesburg Road, Kew 2090, Johannesburg
R28 per night

Rockey Street Backpackers .... (27) (11) 648-8786
34 Regent Street, Yeoville, Johannesburg
R30 per night

Dunkeld West, The Backpackers' Ritz .... (27) (11) 792-1376
6 North Road, Dunkeld West, Johannesburg
R30 per night

The Pink House .... (27) (11) 487-1991
Becker Street, Yeoville, Johannesburg 2192

KUALA LUMPUR

Kuala Lumpur International Youth Hostel .... (60) (3) 273-6870
21 Jalan Kampung Attap, 50460 Kuala Lumpur

LISBON

Pousada de Juventude de Lisboa .... (351) (1) 353-2696
Rua Andrade Corvo 46, 1000 Lisboa
  $2340 per night

HOSTEL SPOTLIGHT

Santa Monica International AYH-Hostel
(310) 393-9913
1436 Second Street, Santa Monica, CA 90401
$17.92 per night for members

  The Santa Monica hostel is a great base for those wishing to explore the Los Angeles area without a car. Convenient to shopping, cafes, restaurants, movie theaters, and just two blocks from the beach, this a great hostel for those who like to have fun. There are regularly scheduled trips to Disneyland and Universal Studios, and the J. Paul Getty Museum is just a bus ride away.

Photo by Ken Geser, courtesy of American Youth Hostels.

Catalazete .... (351) (1) 443-0638
Estrada Marginal, 2780 Oerias
$1700 per night

Los Angeles

Colonial Inn Youth Hostel .... (714) 536-3315
421 Eighth Street, Huntington Beach, CA 92648
Centrally located near Disneyland and beaches

Fullerton Youth Hostel .... (714) 738-3721
1700 North Harbor Boulevard, Fullerton, CA 92635
$9.50–14 per night for members
$12.50–17 per night for non-members

Los Angeles South Bay Youth Hostel .... (310) 831-8109
3601 S Gaffey Street, #613, San Pedro, CA 90733
$9.50–11.50 per night for members
$12.50–14 per night for non-members

Santa Monica International AYH-Hostel .... (310) 393-9913
1436 Second Street, Santa Monica, CA 90401
$17.92 per night for members
See Spotlight

London

The City of London Youth Hostel .... (441) (71) 236-4965
36 Carter Lane, London EC4V 5AD
The hostel has just been completely rebuilt to provide modern furnishing,
central heating and new shower and washing facilities. Sleeping accommo-
dation is in dormitories in striking modern bunks with individual security
lockers.

Hampstead Heath Youth Hostel .... (441) (81) 458-9054
4 Wellgarth Road, Golders Green, London NW11 7HR
See Spotlight

Regency House Hotel .... (441) (71) 637-1804
71 Gower Street, London
Extremely charming bed & breakfast with personable owner

Rotherhithe Youth Hostel .... (441) (71) 232-2114
Salter Road, London SE16 1PP
An ultra-modern building with every facility for groups and individual
travelers alike, including meeting and conference facilities

HOSTEL SPOTLIGHT

Hampstead Heath Youth Hostel
(441) (81) 458-9054
4 Wellgarth Road, Golders Green, London NW11 7HR

This two-hundred-bed hostel located near the Hippodrome is one of seven official AYH hostels located in London. At £12.30 per night for members and £14.50 for non-members, this 'round-the-clock hostel is a great place to stay for those who want to be in London but away from the crowded city center.

Photo by Jim Kennett, courtesy of American Youth Hostels.

Swiss House Hotel .... **(441) (71) 373-2769**
171 Old Brompton Road, South Kensington, London
Close to most of London's main attractions
Winner of the Best Value Bed & Breakfast Award

MADRID

Albergue Juvenil (IYHF) .... **(34) (1) 547-4532**
Calle Sta Cruz de Marcenado No 28, Madrid
950ptas per night

Richard Schirrmann .... **(34) (1) 463-5699**
Casa de Campo, Madrid
950ptas per night

MANCHESTER

Potato Wharf .... **(44) (161) 839-9960**
Castlefield, Manchester M3 4MB
11.5L per night for members
13L per night for non-members

MANILA

Manila International Youth Hostel .... **(63) (2) 832-0680**
4227 Palmas Street, Claudio, Paranaque

CFA Hostel .... **(63) (2) 607 411**
4427 int Old Sta Mesa, Manila

MELBOURNE

Queensberry Hill International Hostel .... **(61) (3) 932 98 599**
78 Howard Street, North Melbourne, Victoria 3051
A$17 per night for members
A$19 per night for non-members

Chapman Gardens .... **(61) (3) 932 83 595**
76 Chapman Street, North Melbourne, Victoria 3051
A$15 per night for members
A$17 per night for non-members

MIAMI

Miami Beach International AYH-Hostel .... **(305) 534-2988**
1438 Washington Avenue, Miami Beach, FL 33139
$33 shared bath/$38 private bath
See Spotlight

Miami Beach International Travelers Hostel .... **(305) 534-0268**
236 Ninth Street, Miami Beach, FL 33139
Budget accommodations for the international traveler

HOSTEL SPOTLIGHT

Miami Beach International AYH-Hostel
(305) 534-2988
1438 Washington Avenue, Miami Beach, FL 33139
$33 shared bath/$38 private bath

*The Miami Beach International Hostel is in the heart of the Old Miami
Beach Art Deco District, which is listed on the National Register of
Historic Places. In its early days, the building was a hangout for Al
Capone's legendary gambling syndicate. The hostel is only two blocks
from the beach and within easy walking distance of ethnic restau-
rants, nightclubs, and boutiques that give Miami Beach a Latin sizzle.
This is where I stay when in Miami Beach.*

*Photo
courtesy of
American
Youth
Hostels.*

Milan

Piero Rotta.. (39) (2) 392 67 095
Via martino Bassi 2 (QT8-San Siro), 20148 Milano
This hostel is open from December 23 to January 13
23,000L per night

Montreal

Auberge de Montrea .... **(514) 843-3317**
1030, rue Mackey, Montreal, Quebec H3G 2HI
$16 per night for members
$20 per night for non-members
$1.75 to rent bedding

Munich

Neuhausen JH .... **(49) (89) 113-1156**
Wendl-Dietrich Strasse 20, 80634 Munich

Pension Clara .... **(49) (89) 348 374**
25 Wilhelmstrasse, Munich
DM60 single/DM85 double

Pension Frank .... **(49) (89) 281 451**
24 Schellingstrasse, Munich
Popular with backpackers
DM65 single/DM85 double
Breakfast is included

Thalkirchen Jugendgastehaus .... **(49) (89) 723-6550**
Meisingstrasse 4, 81379 Munich
DM24-DM36 per night

Nairobi

Nairobi Youth Hostel .... **(254) (2) 721 765**
Ralph Bunche Road, P.O. Box 48661, Nairobi

New York

Allerton House .... **(212) 753-8841**
130 East 57th Street, New York, NY 10022
Women only
$41.99 per night/$59.13 per night with bathroom

New York International AYH Hostel .... **(212) 932-2300**
891 Amsterdam Avenue (W 103rd Street), New York, NY 10025
$20 per night for members/$23 per night for non-members
See Spotlight

The Gershwin .... **(212) 391-4202**
7 East 27th, New York, NY 10016
$20 per night for dormitory accomodations/$65 per night with bathroom
$85 per night for a private room including bathroom and television

Osaka

Hattori Ryokuchi Youth Hostel .... (81) (6) 862-0600
1-3 Hattori-ryokuchi, Toyonaka-shi, Osaka-fu 560
  ¥1,800 per night

HOSTEL SPOTLIGHT

New York International AYH Hostel
(212) 932-2300
891 Amsterdam Avenue (W 103rd Street)
New York, NY 10025
$20 per night for members/$23 per night for non-members

From museums to theaters, from skyscrapers to historic neighborhoods, New York City has it all. The New York International AYH Hostel is in a landmark Victorian Gothic-style building on the city's bustling Upper West Side. Near Central Park and Columbia University, the hostel offers a lively program of walking tours, a hospitality desk staffed by neighborhood volunteers, group outings to concerts and sporting events, and discounts or free tickets to off-Broadway shows, comedy clubs, concerts, and other events.

Photo courtesy of American Youth Hostels.

PARIS

Arpajon .... **(33) (1) 649 02 885**
3 rue Marcel Duhamel, 91290 Arpajon
  45F per night

Cite des Sciences .... **(33) (1) 484 32 411**
24, rue des Sept Arpents, 93310 Le Pre St Gervais
  65F-90F per night

Clichy "Leo Lagrange" .... **(33) (1) 412 72 690**
107 rue Martre, 92110 Clichy
  117F per night for a single
  110F per night for a double

Jules Ferry .... **(33) (1) 435 75 560**
8 Boulevard Jules Ferry, 75011 Paris
  110F per night

Le d'Artagnan .... **(33) (1) 403 23 453**
80 rue Vitruve, 75020 Paris
  110F per night

Relais Europeen Athismons .... **(33) (1) 698 48 139**
Relais Europeen de la Jeuness, 52 avenue Robert Schumann, 91200
Athis Mons (Essonne)
  100F per night

3 Ducks Hostel .... **(33) (1) 484 20 405**
6 pl. E Pernet, Paris
  87F for dormitory housing/107F double

Y & H Hostel .... **(33) (1) 453 50 953**
80 rue Mouffetard, Paris
  Great location and friendly atmosphere
  97F per night per person in a dorm/670F double room for one week

PHILADELPHIA

Bank Street Hostel .... **(800) 392-4678 or (215) 922-0222**
32 S Bank Street, Philadelphia, PA 19106
  $16 per night for members
  $19 per night for non-members

Chamounix Mansion .... **(215) 878-3676**
West Fairmount Park, Philadelphia, PA 19131

QUITO

Hostelling International Quito .... (593) (2) 543 995
Pinto 385 y Reina Victoria, near Amazonas Avenue, Quito, Ecuador

RIO DE JANEIRO

Rio de Janeiro Youth Hostel .... (55) (21) 286-0303
Rua General Dionisio 63, Botatogo, 22271-050 Rio de Janeiro, RJ

Copacabana Praia Youth Hostel .... (55) (21) 236-6472
Rua Tenente Marones de Gusmao 85, Rio de Janeiro
  The best place for the budget traveler in Rio
  Very friendly place near the beach
  Very cheap—$8 single

Hotel Benjamin Constant
Rua Benjamin Constant 10, Rio de Janeiro
  One of the cheapest places to stay in Rio
  Rooms are small and dingy
  $3 single

Hotel Ferreira Viana .... (55) (21) 205-7396
Rua Ferreira Viana 58, Rio de Janeiro
  Very cheap rooms
  $7 single

Hotel Turistico .... (55) (21) 225-9388
Ladeira da Gloria 30, Rio de Janeiro
  Very popular safe and clean budget hotel with foreigners
  $9 single with balcony

ROME

'Foro Italico .... (39) (6) 323-6267
A F Pessina', Viale delle olimpiadi 61, 00194 Rome
  L23,000-L25,000 per night

Pensione Papa Germano .... (39) (6) 486 919
14a Calatafimi, Rome
  L35,000 per night for a single
  L70,000 per night for a double

SAN FRANCISCO

The Essex Hotel ....(800) 45-Essex (USA) or (800) 44-Essex (CA)
684 Ellis Street, San Francisco, CA 94109
An excellent choice for quality accommodations and an unbeatable price of $59 per night for single/$69 per night for double. Centrally located, it is an ideal starting point for San Francisco sightseeing.

San Francisco International Hostel .... (415) 771-7277
Fort Mason, Building 240, San Francisco, CA 94123
$14 per night
See Spotlight

San Francisco International Student Center .... (415) 255-8800
1188 Folsom Street, San Francisco, CA 94103
$13 per night

SANTIAGO

Hostelling International Santiago ....(56) (2) 671-8532
Cienfuegos 151, Santiago de Chile
$10 (US currency) per night for members
$12.50 (US currency) per night for non-members

SAO PAULO

Bela Vista.. (55) (11) 607-3662
Rua Joao Passalacqua 181, Bela Vista, SP

Magdalena Tagliaferro .... (55) (11) 605-3077
Estada Turitica do Jaragua 651,
Pargque Estadual do Jaragua, 05161-0000, Sao Paulo, SP

SEATTLE

Seattle International Youth Hostel .... (206) 622-5443
84 Union Street, Seattle, WA 98101
$16.23 per night for members
$19.23 per night for non-members

SEOUL

Seoul Olympic .... (82) (2) 410-2114
Olympic YH, 88 Bangyi-Dong, Songpa-Ku, Seoul 138-749
W19,800 per night

HOSTEL SPOTLIGHT

San Francisco International Hostel
(415) 771-7277
Fort Mason, Building 240
San Francisco, CA 94123
$14 per night

Ah, San Francisco! Cable cars climbing steep fog-shrouded hills and the famous Golden Gate Bridge make the "city by the bay" one of America's most intriguing and popular destinations. The San Francisco International AYH-Hostel is located at Fort Mason in the Golden Gate National Recreation Area, an urban national park right on the bay. Fort Mason is also home to museums, galleries, and theaters. Fisherman's Wharf, Chinatown, and Ghiradelli Square are all within easy walking distance. This hostel is often booked, especially in summer.

Photo by Ellen Davis, courtesy of American Youth Hostels.

SINGAPORE

Hotel Asia .... **(65) 737-8388**
37 Scotts Road, Singapore
Modest economy hotel
Rooms have air-conditioning
S$125 for a single room

Metropole Hotel .... **(65) 336-3611**
41 Seah Street, Singapore
54-room modest hotel
Rooms have air-conditioning and TV
S$142 per night for a standard room

Metropolitan YMCA, Tanglin Centre .... **(65) 737-7755**
60 Stevens Road, Singapore
Large YMCA with pool, gym, squash courts, and cheap rooms, and food
S$91 per person per night

STOCKHOLM

af Chapman/Skeppsholmen .... **(46) (8) 679-5015**
Vandrarhem 'af Chapman', Skeppsholmen, 11149 Stockholm
135 SEK per night

Skeppsholmen Vastra Bröbanken .... **(46) (8) 679-5017**
Vandrarhem, Skeppsholmen Vastra Bröbanken, 11149 Stockholm
100 SEK per night for members
135 SEK per night for non-members

Backpackers Inn .... **(46) (8) 660-7515**
Banergatan 56, Box 9116, 10272 Stockholm
Open from the end of June to the middle of August

Zinken .... **(46) (8) 616-8100**
Vandrarhem Zinken, Zinkensvag 20, 11741 Stockholm
135 SEK per night

Langholmen .... **(46) (8) 668-0510**
Vandrarhem Langholmen, Kronohaktet, Box 9116, 10272 Stockholm
125 SEK per night for members
160 SEK per night for non-members

SYDNEY

Challis Lodge .... **(61) (2) 358-5422**
21-23 Challis Avenue, Potts Point, Sydney 2011
62 rooms in huge pink Victorian mansion
Very clean and inexpensive
A$32 per night with shared bath/A$42 with private bath

Glebe Point .... **(61) (2) 692-8418**
262 Glebe Point Road, Glebe, New South Wales 2037
A$18 per night for members
A$20 for non-members

Hereford Lodge .... **(61) (2) 660-5577**
51 Hereford Street, Glebe, New South Wales 2037
A$19 per night for members
A$21 per night for non-members

Waratah Central .... **(61) (2) 281-8333**
22-44 Albion Street, Surry Hills, Sydney
182 spacious rooms in this moderately priced hotel
Large pool

TEL AVIV

Tel Aviv Youth Hostel .... **(972) (3) 544-1748**
36 Bnei Dan Street, Tel Aviv 62260
$20 (US currency) per night for a dormitory room
$34 (US currency) per night for a single

TOKYO

Japan YWCA Hostel .... **(81) (3) 326 87 313**
3-1-1 Shinjuku Ichigawa, Sabowara, Tokyo
11 room hostel
Very inexpensive
Women only
¥6,000 per night

Tokyo International Youth Hostel .... **(81) (3) 323 51 107**
21-1 Kagura-kashi, Shinjuku-ku, Tokyo
138 bed hostel
¥2,900 per night

Tokyo YMCA .... **(81) (3) 329 31 919**
7 Mitoshirocho Kanda, Chiyoda-ku, Tokyo
86 room hostel
¥11,330 per night

Yoyogi Youth Hostel .... **(81) (3) 346 79-163**
National Olympics Memorial Youth Center, 31 Yoyogi Kami-zono-cho,
Shibuya-ku, Tokyo 151

Toronto

Hostelling International Toronto .... **(800) 668-4487 or (416) 971-4440**
90 Gerrard Street W, Toronto, Ontario, Canada M5G 1J6
$22.50 per night for members
$26.78 per night for non-members
Dormitory housing

Vancouver

Vancouver Jericho Beach .... **(604) 224-3208**
1515 Discovery Street (Jericho Park), Vancouver, BC, Canada V6R 4K5
$15 per night for members
$19 per night for non-members

Vienna

Myrthengasse (IYHF) .... **(43) (1) 936-3160**
1070 Myrthengasse 7, Neustiftgasse 85, Vienna
130AS per person
Members only

Jungend herberg Lechnerstrasse
Wien, Lechnerstrasse 12

Jungendgastehaus Wein
Brigittenau, 1200 Wien, Friedrich Engelsplatz 24, Vienna

Jungendgastehaus der Stadt Wien
Hutteldorf, Schlossberggasse 8

Hostel Ruthensteiner
Ruthensteiner JH, 1150 Wien, Robert Hameulinggasse 24

WASHINGTON

Hostelling International Washington, DC .... **(202) 737-2333**
1009 11th Street NW, Washington DC 20001
$18 per night for members
$21 per night for non-members

ZURICH

Wollishofen .... **(41) (1) 482-3544**
Mutschellenstrasse 114, Zurich
Busy hostel but very clean
29Fr for members/34Fr for non-members

Marthahaus .... **(41) (1) 251-4550**
36 Zahringerstrasse, Zurich
Dorm rooms for 65Fr single/98Fr double/117Fr triple

HI-AYH COUNCILS ACROSS THE UNITED STATES

T he following is a list of youth hostel council offices throughout the country, where travelers can stock up on information helpful for planning a trip. Council offices sell IYH memberships and hostel directories, and keep a supply of travel-related books and brochures on hand for visitors.

ALASKA

Alaska Council .... **(907) 562-7772**
700 H Street, Anchorage, AK 99501

ARIZONA

Arizona-Southern Nevada Council .... **(520) 774-2731**
23 N Laroux, Flagstaff, AZ 86001

CALIFORNIA

Central California Council .... **(209) 393-0686**
P.O. Box 3645, Merced, CA 95344

Golden Gate Council .... **(415) 863-1444**
425 Divisadero Street, #307, San Francisco, CA 94117

Los Angeles Council .... (310) 393-6263
   Travel Store .... (310) 393-3413
1434 Second Street, Santa Monica, CA 90401

San Diego Council .... (619) 338-9981
500 W Broadway, Suite 218, San Diego, CA 92101

COLORADO

Rocky Mountain Council .... (303) 442-1166
1310 College Avenue, Boulder, CO 80306

CONNECTICUT

Yankee Council .... (202) 236-2027
131 Tremont Street, Hartford, CT 06105

DISTRICT OF COLUMBIA

Potomac Area Council .... (202) 783-0717
   Travel Store .... (202) 783-4943
1108 K Street NW, Washington, DC 20005

FLORIDA

Florida Council .... (500) 443-5294
13819 G Walsingham Road, #223, Largo, FL 34644

GEORGIA

Georgia Council .... (404) 872-8844
P.O. Box 87477, Atlanta, GA 30337

ILLINOIS

Metropolitan Chicago Council .... (312) 327-8114
3036 N Ashland Avenue, Chicago, IL 60657

INDIANA

Indiana Council .... (317) 844-5320
P.O. Box 30048, Indianapolis, IN 46230

IOWA

Northeast Iowa Council .... **(319) 864-3923**
139 W Greene Street, P.O. Box 10, Postville, IA 52162

MASSACHUSETTS

Greater Boston Council .... **(617) 731-5430**
1020 Commonwealth Avenue, Boston, MA 02215

MICHIGAN

Michigan Council .... **(810) 545-0511**
3024 Coolidge, Berkley, MI 48072

MINNESOTA

Minnesota Council .... **(612) 378-3773**
125 SE Main Street, Suite 235, Minneapolis, MN 55417

NEBRASKA

Nebraskaland Council .... **(402) 472-5358**
P.O. Box 81827, Lincoln, NE 68501

NEW YORK

Niagara Frontier Council .... **(716) 852-5222**
1616 Lynnwood Avenue, P.O. Box 1110, Buffalo, NY 14205

Syracuse Council .... **(315) 472-5788**
535 Oak Street, Syracuse, NY 13203

Hudson-Mohawk Council .... **(919) 286-1477**
P.O. Box 7066, Albany, NY 12225

NORTH CAROLINA

Piedmont Council .... **(910) 286-1477**
P.O. Box 10766, Winston-Salem, NC 27108

Ohio

Northeast Ohio Council .... **(216) 467-8771**
6093 Sanford Road, Peninsula, OH 44624

Toledo Area Council .... **(419) 841-4510**
P.O. Box 352736, Toledo, OH 43635-2736

Oregon

Oregon Council .... **(503) 236-3380**
3031 Hawthorne Boulevard SE, Portland, OR 97214

Pennsylvania

Delaware Valley Council .... **(215) 925-6004**
24 S Third Street, Philadelphia, PA 19147

Pittsburgh Council .... **(412) 362 8181**
5604 Solway Street, Room 202, Pittsburgh, PA 15217

Texas

Bluebonnet Council .... **(713) 520-5332**
2715 Bissonnet, #213, Houston, TX 77005

North Texas Council .... **(214) 350-4294**
3530 Forset Lane, #127, Dallas, TX 75234

Southwest Texas Council .... **(512) 444-2300**
2200 S Lakeshore Boulevard, Austin, TX 78741

Washington

Washington State Council .... **(206) 281-7306**
419 Queen Anne Avenue N, #101, Seattle, WA 98109

Wisconsin

Wisconsin Council .... **(414) 961-2525**
5900 N Port Washington Road, Suite 146, Milwaukee, WI 53217

WORLDWIDE HOSTS

Servas is yet another option for lodging. Servas is an international organization that joins together hosts and travelers. There are members all over the world. As a traveler you will stay for free in the home of a host. It is an opportunity for both of you to learn about each other's culture. There is an application process, interview, and screening. For an application contact:

U.S. Servas Committee
11 John Street, Room 407, New York, NY 10038 .... (212) 267-0252

INTERNATIONAL TOURIST OFFICES

The following offices will help you with your trip by providing valuable information about their countries. This information includes maps, lodging, exchange rates, sights, and more. Their services are free.

Australian Tourism Commission
100 Park Avenue, 25th Floor, New York, NY 10017 .... (212) 687-6300

Austrian National Tourist Office
P.O. Box 1142, Times Square, New York, NY 10108-1142 (212) 944-6880
500 N Michigan Avenue, Suite 1950, Chicago, IL 60611 .. (312) 644-5556
11601 Wilshire Blvd, Suite 2480, Los Angeles, CA 90025 (310) 477-3332
2 Bloor Street E, Suite 3330, Toronto, ON M4W 1A8 .... (416) 367-3381
101 Oest rue Sherbrooke, Montreal, PQ H3A 2R7 .... (514) 849-3709

Brazilian Tourist Office
16 W 46th Street, 2nd Floor, New York, NY 10036 .... (212) 730-1010

British Tourist Authority
551 5th Avenue, New York, NY 10176 .... (800) 462-2748

Scandinavian Tourist Board
655 3rd Avenue, New York, NY 10017 .... (212) 949-2333

European Trade Commission
630 5th Avenue, Suite 565, New York, NY 10111 .... (212) 307-1200

French Government Tourist Office
444 Madison Avenue, New York, NY 10022 .... (212) 838-7800
676 N Michigan Avenue, Suite 3360, Chicago, IL 60611 .. (312) 751-7800
9454 Wilshire Blvd, Suite 715, Beverly Hills, CA 90212 .. (310) 271-2358
30 St. Patrick Street, Suite 700, Toronto, ON M5G 3A3 ... (416) 593-4723
1981 McGill College Avenue, Montreal, PQ H3A 2W9 ... (514) 288-4264

German National Tourist Office
122 E 42nd Street, 52nd Floor, New York, NY 10168 ...... (212) 661-7200
11766 Wilshire Blvd, Suite 750, Los Angeles, CA 980025 (310) 575-9799
175 Bloor Street E, North Tower, Suite 604,
Toronto, ON M4W 3R8 .... (416) 968-1570

Greek National Tourist Organization
645 5th Avenue, New York, NY 10022 .... (212) 421-5777

Hong Kong Tourist Association
590 5th Avenue, New York, NY 10036 .... (212) 869-5008

Irish Tourist Board
345 Park Avenue, New York, NY 10154 .... (800) 223-6470
(212) 418-0800

Japan National Tourist Information
Rockefeller Center, Suite 1250, New York, NY 10020 ...... (212) 757-5640
165 University Avenue, Toronto, ON M5H 3B8 .... (416) 366-7140

Korea National Tourism Corporation
2 Executive Drive, Suite 750, Fort Lee, NJ 07024 .... (212) 688-7543

Mexican Government Tourism Office
405 Park Avenue, Suite 1401 New York, NY 10022 .... (212) 838-2949

Netherlands National Tourist Office
355 Lexington Ave, Suite 1401, New York, NY 10017 .... (800) 95-DUTCH
(212) 370-7360
255 N Michigan Avenue, Suite 326, Chicago, IL 60601 .... (312) 819-0300
25 Adelaide Street, Toronto, ON M5C 1Y2 .... (416) 363-1577

New Zealand Travel Commission
666 Fifth Avenue, 37th Floor, New York, NY 10103 .... (212) 529-0871
12400 Wilshire Blvd, Suite 1150, Los Angeles, CA 90025 (310) 207-1145

Spanish National Tourist Office
666 5th Avenue, 35th Floor, New York, NY 10002 .... (212) 265-8822
845 N Michigan Avenue, Suite 915E, Chicago, IL 60611 . (312) 642-1992
8383 Wilshire Blvd, Suite 946, Beverly Hill, CA 90211 .... (213) 658-7188
1221 Brikell Avenue, Miami, FL 33131 .... (305) 358-1992
112 Bloor Street W, Toronto, ON M58 1M8 .... (416) 961-3131

USEFUL ORGANIZATIONS

The Center for Global Education .... **(612) 330-1159**
2211 Riverside Avenue, Minneapolis, MN 55454
Third world tour operator

Council Charter .... **(800) 223-7402**
The oldest charter company in the United States

Elderhostel .... **(617) 426-7788**
75 Federal Street, Boston, MA 02110-1941
Study programs in the U.S. and Europe for people over 60

Experiment in International Living ...... **(800) 451-4465 or (802) 257-7751**
P.O. Box 676, Battleboro, VT 05302

London Student Travel .... **(441) (71) 730-3402**
52 Gosvenor Gardens, London WC1, England

STA Travel (Student Travel Association) .... **(800) 777-0112**
Over 100 offices worldwide

Travel CUTS (Canadian University Travel Services) .... **(416) 979-2406**
187 College Street, Toronto, ON M5T 1P7

Volunteers for Peace .... **(802) 259-2759**
43 Tiffany Road, Belmont, VT 05730

COUNCIL TRAVEL OFFICES

The Council on International Educational Exchange (CIEE) operates a network of retail travel offices across the country providing low-cost flights, rail passes, language courses, insurance, and books.

130 E University Drive, Suite A, Tempe, AZ 85281 .... (602) 966-3544
2486 Channing Way, Berkeley, CA 94704 .... (510) 848-8604
9500 Gilman Dr, UCSD Price Center, La Jolla, CA 92093 ... (619) 452-0630
1800 Pal Verde Avenue, Suite F, Long Beach, CA 90815 . (714) 527-7950
10904 Lindbrook Drive, Los Angeles, CA 90024 .... (310) 208-3551
394 University Avenue, Suite 200, Palo Alto, CA 94301 . (415) 325-3888
953 Garnet Avenue, San Diego, CA 92109 .... (619) 270-6401
530 Bush Street, San Francisco, CA 94108 .... (415) 421-3473
919 Irving Street, Suite 102, San Francisco, CA 94122 .... (415) 566-6222
1138 13th Street, Boulder, CO 80302 .... (303) 447-8101
Yale Co-op E, 77 Broadway, New Haven CT 06520 .... (203) 562-5335
3300 M Street NW, 2nd Floor, Washington, DC 20007 ... (202) 377-6464
9100 S Dadeland Blvd, Suite 320, Miami, FL 33156 .... (305) 670-9261

1561 N Decatur Road, Atlanta, GA 30307 .... (404) 377-9997
1153 N Dearborn Street, Chicago, IL 60610 .... (312) 951-0585
1634 Orrington Avenue, Evanston, IL 60201 .... (708) 475-5070
6363 St. Charles Avenue, Joseph Dana Center,
   Loyola University, New Orleans, LA 70118 .... (504) 866-1767
44 Main Street, Amherst, MA 01002 .... (617) 266-7926
729 Boylston Street, Suite 201, Boston, MA 02116 .... (617) 266-1926
Stratton Student Center, MIT, 12 Eliot St, Cambridge, MA (617) 225-2555
1220 S University Drive, Ann Arbor, MI .... (313) 998-0200
1501 University Ave SE, Room 300,
   Minneapolis, MN 55414 .... (612) 379-2323
205 E 42nd Street, New York, NY 10017 .... (212) 661-1450
895 Amsterdam Avenue Street, New York, NY 10025 ..... (212) 666-4177
148 W 4th Street, New York, 10012 .... (212) 254-2525
703 9th Street, Suite B-2, Durham, NC 27705 .... (919) 286-4664
8 E 13th Avenue, Columbus, OH 43201 .... (614) 294-8696
715 SW Morrison, Suite 600, Portland, OR 43201 .... (503) 228-1900
3606A Chestnut Steet, Philadelphia, PA 19104 .... (215) 382-0343
171 Angell Street, Suite 212, Providence, RI 02906 .... (401) 331-5810
2000 Guadalupe Street, Austin, TX 78705 .... (512) 472-4931
6715 Hillcrest, Dallas, TX 75205 .... (214) 363-9941
1314 NE 43rd Street, Suite 210, Seattle, WA 98105 .... (206) 632-2448
219 Broadway Avenue E, Suite 17, WA 98102 .... (206) 329-4567

LIST OF RECOMMENDED TRAVEL BOOKS

These books usually can be found at your local bookstore, library, or one of the travel bookstores listed in the next section.

The Asia Employment Program
A comprehensive guide to teaching English in Japan, South Korea, Taiwan, Indonesia, Thailand, and China. Available only from Progressive Media, P.O. Box 45220, Seattle, WA 98145-0220.

The Bed & Breakfast Directory
This book provides details on over 1,000 B & Bs in the United States and Canada. A handy book when traveling to North America.

The Berkeley Guides
A travel series designed for the budget traveler.

The Best Pubs of Great Britain
One of my favorite books.

Birnbaum's Guides
These books focus on the moderate price range.

Cheap Sleeps/Cheap Eats in London
A great book if you are going to London.

Cheap Sleeps/Cheap Eats in Paris
A great book if you are going to Paris.

China Solo: A Guide to Independent Travel in China
Ideal for courier travelers.

The Cruise and Travel Employment Program
A comprehensive guide to finding employment in the cruise and travel industries. Available only from Progressive Media, P.O. Box 85180, Seattle, WA 98145-1180.

The Eastern Europe Employment Program
Another in this series of outstanding employment programs. This guide covers job opportunities primarily teaching English in the Czech and Slovak Republics, Hungary, and Poland. Available from Progressive Media, P.O. Box 45760, Seattle, WA 98145-0760.

Europe For Free
A great book with lots of free things to do in Europe.

Europe for One: A Complete Guide for Solo Travelers
Ideal book for courier travelers.

Europe: Where the Fun is
A guide to where the action is in Europe.

Fielding's Travel Guides
Plenty of information in these books, however, much of it is in the expensive range. Look for his Budget Europe *guides.*

Fodor's Travel Guides
The books highlight individual cities and countries. This could be of more help if you are only planning on seeing one or two cities on your trip.

Ford's Freighter Travel Guide

Frommer's Guides
An excellent choice for budget-minded travelers.

Gault Millau Guides
Refreshing, critical, and honest remarks are the trademark for this series.

Going Places: The Guide to Travel Guides
A great book that lists and describes thousands of travel guides. There are comprehensive reviews on all the popular guides as well as many that you never heard of.

Guide to Greater London: Hotels, Pubs, and Restaurants

Hippocrene Books, Inc.
They publish travel reference books, travel guides, maps, and foreign language dictionaries.

The Insult Dictionary: How to Give 'Em Hell in Five Different Languages
For those times when you need to chew someone out in French, German, Italian, Spanish, and English.

John Muir Publications
They publish a whole line of travel books.

Lonely Planet Publications
They offer a large selection of travel books.

The Lover's Dictionary: How to be Amourous in Five Delectable Languages
For those times when you need to say something romantic in French, German, Italian, Spanish, and English.

Moon Handbooks
This series is for the adventurous. Public transportation is the primary mode of travel for the users of these books.

Passport to Discount Travel
A great book that will help you save money.

Traveler's Hotline Directory
This book lists over 12,000 toll free phone numbers for the travel industry.

Vagabonding USA: A Guide to Independent Travel
One of my personal favorites. This book is a must if you are traveling around the United States.

TRAVEL BOOKSTORES AND MAIL ORDER COMPANIES

Adventures & Delights
414 K Street, Anchorage, AK 99501 .... (907) 276-8282

Basically Books
46 Waianuenue Avenue, Hilo, HI 96720 .... (808) 961-0144

Book Passage
51 Tamal Vista Boulevard, Corte Madera, CA 94925 .... (415) 927-0960

California Map & Travel Center
3211 Pico Boulevard, Santa Monica, CA 90405 .... (310) 829-6277

The Complete Traveler
3207 Filmore Street, San Francisco, CA 94123 .... (415) 923-1511

Complete Traveller
199 Madison Avenue, New York, NY 10016 .... (212) 685-9007

Delorme's Map Store
P.O. Box 928, Freeport, ME 04042 .... (207) 865-4171

Distant Lands
62 S Raymond Avenue, Old Pasadena, CA 91105 .... (818) 449-3220

Ed & Fred's Traveler's Store
1007 W Webster Ave, Chicago, IL 60614 .... (312) 477-6220

Easy Going
1385 Shattuck Avenue, Berkeley, CA 94109 .... (510) 843-3533
1617 Locust Street, Walnut Creek, CA 94596 .... (510) 947-6660

Forsyth Travel Bookstore
9154 W 57th Street, Shawnee Mission, KS 66201 .... (913) 384-3440

4 Corners Map & Travel Shop
1887 W Market Street, Akron, OH 43313 .... (330) 869-6277

Geographia Map & Travel Bookstore
4000 Riverside Drive, Burbank, CA 91505 .... (818) 848-1414

Going Places Map & Travel Bookstore
2860 University Avenue, Madison, WI 53705 .... (608) 233-1920

Gulliver's Travel Bookshop
609 Bloor Street W, Toronto, ON M6G 1K5 .... (416) 537-7700

Hagstrom Map & Travel Center
57 W 43rd Street, New York, NY 10036 .... (212) 398-1222

Hannslik & Wegner International Bookstore
20 Railroad Place, Westport, CT 06880 .... (203) 454-7750

The Happy Wanderer
320 N Highway 89A, Sedona, AZ 86336 .... (520) 282-4690

International Travel Service
3063 Beacon Avenue S, Seattle, WA 98144 .... (206) 860-5008

Jet-Setter
66 Laurier Street W, Montreal, PQ H2T 2N4 .... (514) 271-5058

Kopi—A Traveler's Cafe
5317 N Clark, Chicago, IL 60640 .... (312) 989-5674

Le Travel Store
715 4th Avenue, San Diego, CA 92101 .... (619) 544-0005

The Map Center
63 Washington Street, Santa Clara, CA 95050 .... (408) 296-6277
2440 Bancroft Way, Berkeley, CA 94704 .... (510) 841-6277

Map Centre Inc.
2611 University Avenue, San Diego, CA 92104 .... (619) 291-3830

The Map Man
17 W Nicholai, Hicksville, NY 11801 .... (516) 931-8404

The Map Shop
5-B E Coffee Street, Greenville, SC 29602 .... (803) 271-6277

The Map Store
200 S 6th Street, Minneapolis, MN 55402 .... (612) 339-4117
5821 Karric Square Drive, Dublin, OH 43016 .... (614) 792-6277
30 E 7th Street, Saint Paul, MN 55101 .... (614) 227-6277
1636 Eye Street NW, Washington, DC 20006 .... (202) 628-2608

Maps Unlimited
899 Broadway, Denver, CO 80203 .... (303) 623-4299

Metsker Maps of Bellevue
1645 140th Avenue NE, Bellevue, WA 98005 .... (206) 746-3200

Metsker Maps of Seattle
702 1st Avenue, Seattle, WA 98104 .... (206) 623-8747

One Savvy Traveler
310 S Michigan, Chicago, IL 60604 .... (312) 913-9800

Pacific Travellers Supply
12 W Anapanu Street, Santa Barbara, CA 93101 .... (805) 963-4438

Passenger Stop—Your Travel Store
740 Dulaney Valley Rd, Towson, MD 21208 .... (800) 261-5888
(410) 821-5888

Phileas Fogg's Books
87 Stanford Shopping Center, Palo Alto, CA 94304 .... (415) 327-1754

Powell's Travel Store
701 SW Sixth Avenue, Portland, OR 97204 .... (503) 228-1108

Rand McNally Map & Travel Store
3333 Bristol Street, Suite 2231, Costa Mesa, CA 92626 .... (714) 545-9907
243 Horton Plaza, San Diego, CA 92101 .... (619) 234-3341
595 Market Street, San Francisco, CA 94105 .... (415) 777-3131
3101 PGA Boulevard, Palm Beach Gardens, FL 33410 .... (407) 775-7602
444 N Michigan Avenue, Chicago, IL 60601 .... (312) 321-1751
452 Oakbrook Center, Oak Brook, IL 60521 .... (708) 571-3006
G101 Woodfield Mall, Schaumburg, IL 60173 .... (708) 995-9606
84 State Street, Boston, MA 02109 .... (617) 720-1125
7101 Democracy Boulevard, Bethesda, MD 20817 .... (301) 365-6277
Sommerset Collection .... (810) 643-7470
2801 W Big Beaver Road J226, Troy, MI 48084
2423 St. Louis Galleria, St. Louis, MO 63117 .... (314) 863-3555
1200 Morris Turnpike, The Mall at Short Hills .... (201) 319-1800
Short Hills, NJ 07078
150 E 52nd Street, New York, NY 10022 .... (212) 758-7488

1650 Market Street, Suite 100, Philadelphia, PA 19103 .... (215) 563-1101
211 North Park Center, Dallas, TX 75225 .... (214) 987-9941
5015 Westheimer, Houston, TX 77056 .... (713) 960-9846
7988 Tysons Corner Center, McLean, VA 22102 .... (703) 556-8688
150 S Wacker, Chicago, IL 60606 .... (312) 332-2009

The Savvy Traveler
310 South Michigan, Chicago, IL 60604 .... (312) 913-9800

Thomas Brothers Maps
521 W 6th Street, Los Angeles, CA 90017 .... (213) 627-4018
17731 Cowan, Irvine, CA 92714 .... (714) 863-1984
550 Jackson Street, San Francisco, CA 94133 .... (415) 981-7520

Travel & Nature
59 Water Street, Exeter, NH 03833 .... (603) 772-5573

Travel Books & Language Center
4931 Cordell Avenue, Bethesda, MD 20814 .... (301) 951-8533

The Travel Bug
2667 W Broadway, Vancouver, BC V6K 2G2 .... (604) 737-1122

Travel Collection
8015 Shoal Creek Blvd, Suite 1188, Austin, TX 78757 ...... (512) 454-7151

The Travel Emporium
210 Ventura Boulevard, Woodland Hills, CA 91364 .... (818) 592-0718

The Travel Gallery
1007 Manhattan Avenue, Manhattan Beach, CA 90266 ... (310) 379-9199

Explore
620 W Lincolnway, Ames, IA 50010 .... (515) 232-8843

Traveler's Bookcase
8375 W 3rd Street, Los Angeles, CA 90048 .... (313) 655-0575

Traveler's Depot
1655 Garnet Avenue, San Diego, CA 92109 .... (619) 483-1421

Traveller's Bookstore
22 W 52nd Street, New York, NY 10020 .... (800) 755-TRAVEL
(212) 664-0995

Travel Merchandise Mart
1425 K Street NW, Washington, DC 20005 .... (703) 415-1424

The Travel Store
56 1/2 N Santa Cruz Avenue, Los Gatos, CA 95030 .... (408) 354-9909

Traveling Books and Maps
4001 S. Decatur #34 Las Vegas, NV 89103 .... (800) 240-1774

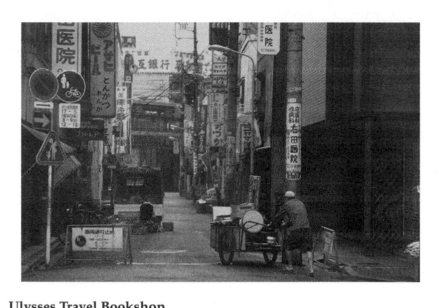

Ulysses Travel Bookshop
4176 Saint Denis, Montreal, PQ H2W 2M5 .... (514) 843-9447
4 Rana Lavasqua, Quebec City, PQ G1R 2B1 .... (418) 529-5349
101 Yorkville Avenue, Toronto, ON M5R 1C1 .... (416) 323-3609

Venture Map & Globe
2525 W Anderson, Austin, TX 78757 .... (512) 452-2326

Wanderlust
1929 W 4th Street, Vancouver, BC V6J 1M7 .... (604) 739-2182

Wide World Books & Maps
1911 N 45th Street, Seattle, WA 98103 .... (206) 634-3453

Wide World of Maps
2626 W Indian School Road, Phoenix, AZ 85017 .... (602) 279-2323

Wide World of Maps
1334 S Country Club Drive, Mesa, AZ 85210 .... (602) 844-1134

Woodruff & Blum Booksellers
Samson Mall, P.O. Box 118, Lake Louise, Alberta, TOL 1E0 ... (403) 522-3842

World Wide Books & Maps
736 Granville Street, Vancouver, BC V6Z 1G3 .... (604) 687-3320

INDEX

ORDER FORM
(This form may be photocopied)

"Enterprising travelers should consider flying as a courier. Check out Mark I. Field's travel handbook."
—*Let's Go Travel Guides*

To order additional copies of *The Courier Air Travel Handbook*, just fill out the form below or call:

(800) 807-3030
(Credit card orders only)

Send check or money order with this form to:
PERPETUAL PRESS
P.O. Box 45628
Seattle, WA 98145-0628

____ copies of the Courier Handbook @ $9.95 each [＿＿＿]

Shipping and handling [＿＿＿]
($2.00 for the first book, $1.00 for each additional copy)

TOTAL [＿＿＿]

SHIPPING INFORMATION

Name: _____

Address: _____

City/State/Zip: _____

Phone: _____